T0330544

ROUTLEDGE LIBRARY EDITIONS:
ACCOUNTING HISTORY

Volume 21

FACTORY ACCOUNTS

FACTORY ACCOUNTS

JOHN WHITMORE

Routledge
Taylor & Francis Group

LONDON AND NEW YORK

First published in 1984 by Garland Publishing, Inc.

This edition first published in 2021
by Routledge
2 Park Square, Milton Park, Abingdon, Oxon OX14 4RN

and by Routledge
52 Vanderbilt Avenue, New York, NY 10017

Routledge is an imprint of the Taylor & Francis Group, an informa business

British Library Cataloguing in Publication Data
A catalogue record for this book is available from the British Library

ISBN: 978-0-367-33564-9 (Set)
ISBN: 978-1-00-304636-3 (Set) (ebk)
ISBN: 978-0-367-49459-9 (Volume 21) (hbk)
ISBN: 978-1-00-304635-6 (Volume 21) (ebk)

Publisher's Note
The publisher has gone to great lengths to ensure the quality of this reprint but points out that some imperfections in the original copies may be apparent.

Disclaimer
The publisher has made every effort to trace copyright holders and would welcome correspondence from those they have been unable to trace.

Factory Accounts

John Whitmore

GARLAND PUBLISHING, INC.
NEW YORK & LONDON   1984

For a complete list of the titles in this series
see the final pages of this volume.

Library of Congress Cataloging in Publication Data

Whitmore, John.
Factory accounts.

(Accounting history and the development of a profession)
1. Factories—Accounting—History.   2. Cost accounting
—History.   I. Title.   II. Series.
HF5686.M3W55   1984   657'.867   83-49447
ISBN 0-8240-6314-7 (alk. paper)

The volumes in this series are printed on
acid-free, 250-year-life paper.

Printed in the United States of America

Editor's Note

*I*n 1906–07 John Whitmore published a series of articles in *The Journal of Accountancy.* They were based on four lectures with the title of "Factory Accounts" given at the School of Commerce, Accounts and Finance at New York University in the winter of 1905–06. Writing thirty years later, Edwards commented that Whitmore provides in these articles "quite as detailed and good an analysis as we get today."[1]

In the winter of 1908 Whitmore delivered another lecture at New York University and it dealt with the subject of shoe factory cost accounts. It gives a clear account of standard costing and has been described as the "first of its kind to appear in accounting literature."[2]

This volume reprints these classic articles by Whitmore and it also contains some of his other works on cost accounting.

[1]R. S. Edwards, "Some Notes on the Early Literature and Development of Cost Accounting in Great Britain," VI, *The Accountant*, September 11, 1937; reprinted in B. S. Yamey, ed., *The Historical Development of Accounting* (New York: Arno Press, 1978). Whitmore's articles also were reprinted in *The Accountant* in 1906 and 1907.

[2]J. Hugh Jackson, "A Quarter-Century of Cost-Accounting Progress," *N.A.C.A. Bulletin*, June 1, 1947 as quoted by David Solomons, "The Historical Development of Costing," in David Solomons, ed., *Studies in Cost Analysis*, 2nd ed., (Homewood, Illinois: Richard D. Irwin, Inc., 1968), p. 37. Jackson is quoting W. B. Macfarland.

Contents[*]

*All articles originally appeared in *The Journal of Accountancy*

Factory Accounting as Applied to Machine Shops

Factory Accounting as Applied to Machine Shops.

I.

The present articles upon machine shop accounts are based upon four lectures given before the School of Commerce, Accounts, and Finance, of New York University last winter. These lectures were given under the title of "Factory Accounting," and it is as an aspect, or a particular development, of factory accounting in general, that machine shop accounts in particular were treated of. Or it may be said that machine shop accounts were chosen for the purpose of furnishing a convenient means of introduction to the general principles of factory accounting, because the particular methods developed in them have a wide application in other industries.

The reason for this is of course plain. A large part of the equipment of every factory is mechanical, and the operation of the machinery is necessarily to some extent recorded by methods parallel to those used to record the operation of the machinery in machine shops. The operations themselves are different and the materials worked are different, and the accounting methods are specialized in each industry in a manner that may have little relationship to any other, except that they always embody the principle of double-entry bookkeeping and always follow the operations as closely as available data will permit. But in every industry we have the accounting which is necessary to the operation of machinery; that is, if the standard of economy attained in its operation is to be determined, or if the cost of its operation is to be traced to particular products, and the methods of this accounting can best be made plain in connection with the operations of machine shops themselves.

Again in every factory there are repair operations which are, generally speaking, either machine shop operations or carpenter shop operations, to which the accounting methods of machine shops conform; while in the larger factories of every industry there are larger or smaller machine shops for construction and repair work.

And generally speaking there is in every factory the development and utilization of power, the accounting for which is largely an engineering problem, and may best be considered in connection with the industry in which the power equipment is produced and over which the mechanical engineer especially presides.

Again the storehouses of the various industries are subject to many conditions which seem peculiar to themselves, but which are rarely radically different from the conditions existing in machine shop storehouses.

So that it seems plain that in every industry a thorough accounting must be in part accomplished by the methods necessary in machine shops, while in every industry there must be made departures to faithfully follow operations which are unlike machine shop operations. A clear perception of the similarities and the dissimilarities is one of the great essentials to the practice of factory accounting. The fundamental principle is always the same, namely, the principle of making a record sufficiently full to constitute a clear accounting for the factory expenditure; and the object of the accounts is always the same, namely, to eliminate waste from the operations. This then may be said to be the purpose of all factory accounting: to produce records in which waste shall be plainly shown as waste.

It cannot be perfectly accomplished, because waste in factories is of too complex, or rather of too obscure and elusive a character. To perfectly economical production there are two things principally necessary, and the vital importance of neither one nor the other seems ever fully appreciated—the first is the full utilization of factory capacity, and the second the development of mutual interest between employer and employee. The first of these is quite properly a subject for factory accounting, and the second at least to the extent that accounting may help to determine the true conditions of mutual interest.

It may almost be said that economy in production is attained if this single condition is fulfilled, namely, that factory capacity be fully utilized. This does not mean merely that every machine shall be in constant operation, but that it shall be constantly operated to the maximum advantage. If materials worked upon are spoiled the factory capacity that has been employed upon them is wasted. If a machine is employed upon less important work than that for which it was designed and is fitted, its capacity is partly wasted. If labor or management is inefficient and a machine is slackly operated, or the processes are ill arranged, capacity is wasted.

When it is borne in mind that the capacity of the business organization is limited by the capacity of the factory, and that machinery and organization expenses constitute an ever increasing percentage of the cost of the product, the vital importance of the fullest possible utilization of factory capacity begins to be plain. And it is useful to bear in mind that it is through the study of the factory capacity, and through the accounting that may be set up in relation to it, that the most perfect test of efficiency is arrived at.

The aim of the modern developments of machinery has been to reduce the labor required in the immediate processes of manufacturing. That is to say, in order to manufacture goods of a certain class it is found to be most economical to first expend labor in the production of machinery, and to expend labor very freely in the production of machinery of high efficiency, and then to expend, relatively to what would otherwise have been necessary, very little labor in producing the goods by the operation of the machinery. The investment in machinery and the expenses, other than labor, attaching to its operation are systematically increased. Everything then depends upon whether the plant is so operated as to secure the final economy that has been aimed at. To provide that it shall be so operated a more or less expensive organization has to be created. Two heavy expenses are thus incurred: First, machinery expense; second, organization expense. But if the machinery is fitted for its purpose and the organization is efficient, a product is obtained at a lower final cost than is possible under conditions which do not include these large preliminary outlays.

It is these altered conditions that makes necessary the modern systematic factory accounting. The old methods are obviously inadequate, and as means of determining costs are simply a failure, because accurate cost figures cannot, under the newer conditions, be arrived at by them.

In the first of the lectures alluded to somewhat extended reference was made to two works. The first is Garcke & Fells' "Factory Accounting," published in London in 1887, and the second a series of six articles written by Mr. A. Hamilton Church and published in the *Engineering Magazine* from July to December, 1901, under the title of "The Proper Distribution of the Factory Expense Burden." Messrs. Garcke & Fells' book was probably the first serious attempt to give systematic accuracy to factory records by embodying in them the principle of double-entry bookkeeping, and it also went far to indicate the varied and practical uses of modern factory accounting. Mr. Church's articles, written with an engineer's knowledge of modern machine shop conditions, constitute an exceedingly valuable and relatively exhaustive essay upon the subject indicated by their title.

Messrs. Garcke & Fells described the methods prevailing at the time their book was written. They said that some manufacturers added a percentage to "Prime Cost," i. e., the cost of material and direct labor, and some added one percentage to materials and another to direct labor, and some a single percentage to direct labor. They speak also of some existing use of machine rates, i. e., charges per hour for the use of the various machines, and they outline a method of determining and using machine rates. According to this method there were taken into consideration the original cost of the machine, its estimated hours of working life, its cost of maintenance, and its residual value; and a "Plant Ledger" was to be kept with an account for each machine, and these accounts were to be charged with original cost and with maintenance expenditure, and credited with the machine rates charged in the cost accounts, treating then the balances of each machine account as the present value of the machine. It will be seen that this involved charging all repairs to the capital plant accounts in the general books, and writing off depreciation rates which would cover both repairs and the depreciation which goes on in spite of repairs.

Messrs. Garcke & Fells' preference was evidently for the use of these machine rates to charge cost accounts with the expenses of the maintenance and depreciation of the machines actually employed in production, and as to all other factory general charges to periodically ascertain their total and to distribute this as a percentage upon the direct labor expenditure, charging the various cost accounts accordingly.

As has already been said, there is in modern factory development, along with the reduction of the direct cost of processes, a tendency to increased indirect or organization expenses; and with the reduction of direct labor there is inevitably increased plant expense. At the time Messrs. Garcke & Fells published their book they said that many manufacturers were still content to take out "Prime Cost" merely, i. e., only the expense of materials and direct labor. Evidently these manufacturers were following methods that belonged to earlier conditions of the manufacturing industries when machine and organization expenses were relatively small factors in the cost of production, and more progressive manufacturers were giving some careful consideration to the manner in which machine and organization expenses actually entered into the costs of the various products. As then machine tools were more highly developed, and as factories were organized on a still larger scale, it gradually became plain that with only the cost of materials and direct labor actually determined, and with ever increasing items of machine and organization expenses roughly and arbitrarily distributed, the cost figures arrived at meant little or nothing.

If manufacturers generally were slow to realize the effect of the changed conditions upon necessary methods of calculating costs, it had been noted elsewhere and plainly set out. Professor Davidson, of the University of New Brunswick, in a book entitled "The Bargain Theory of Wages," published in 1898, said: "Labor cost without machinery is a different thing from labor cost with machinery. We must include in the real labor cost of production in machinery industry the cost of the labor-saving machine, that is, the expenses of its working, and the contribution to the sinking fund to replace the machine. Machinery has to a large extent reduced the nominal labor cost, but statistics are lacking to show how far the real and complete labor cost has been reduced."

The necessities of the new situation, as far as machine shops are concerned, were very fully considered and dealt with in Mr. Church's articles in the *Engineering Magazine,* already referred to. Mr. Church deals with the various older methods of distributing indirect expenses, and makes very plain, as indeed it is not difficult to do, their inadequacy and their random character in relation to modern shop conditions. He then proceeds to develop a machine rate that shall express the hourly cost of the machine as nearly as possible in the same way that a workman's hourly rate expresses the cost of his labor. This is done by simply compiling the cost of providing a given machine, together with all its accessories, and under working conditions. The capital investment is represented in this cost by an interest charge. The annual expense arrived at is reduced to an expense per hour. Then the time a machine is taken up by a given job is recorded, and the job is charged with so many hours at so much per hour.

It is proposed to carefully consider two features of Mr. Church's plan. The first is the inclusion of interest on investment of capital as part of the cost of production; and the second is the "Supplementary Rate" by which Mr. Church takes up and charges against the products the expenses running against the machines in idle hours.

The first of these deserves careful consideration because it has not been customary to include interest on capital in cost of production, and the idea of doing so is one that both manufacturers and accountants commonly feel some reluctance to adopt. Yet its inclusion is essential to an accurate distinction between varying costs.

Nor apparently has interest on capital been omitted from the cost of production without some careful consideration. Messrs. Garcke & Fells say: "The establishment charges and interest on capital should not in any case form part of the cost of production—there is no advantage in distributing these items over the various transactions." And again: "The principals of a business acquainted with its details can always judge what percentage of gross profit upon cost is necessary to cover fixed establishment charges." As related to interest on capital this is true under simple conditions, and becomes very doubtful under the complex conditions of a large plant with a varied equipment and a varied output. It is obvious that in different industries there is a very different ratio between a given rate of interest upon the capital employed and the other costs of production. In other words, in order to pay a given rate of return upon the capital invested a much larger percentage of profit is necessary in some industries than in others. Every manufacturer knows what rate of profit he must make in order to get a certain return upon his capital. Suppose now that a large plant includes what elsewhere exists as several separate industries, foundries, forges, machine shops, carpenter shops and so on, and suppose that the output of these departments is not always combined in something like similar proportions in the finished product, but that the product may even occasionally be that of a single de-

253

7

partment. To apply always an average percentage of profit as necessary may be to introduce into a competing price on certain articles a figure that does not belong to the single industry in which these articles are produced and which does not exist for competitors who are engaged in the single industry. Or suppose that a concern has two competitors, one making one class of goods and another making another class, and that these two competitors employ capital in different proportions to output. Each knows "what percentage of profit upon cost is necessary," and in the two cases it is not the same. But the single concern producing both classes of goods knows only one percentage. It is plain where the advantage lies in accurate knowledge of costs and in making competing prices.

Again, the same goods made with equal economy by two concerns should naturally have the same cost price. But if one rents what another owns, perhaps by means of having borrowed money upon which it pays interest, either one must exclude rent from its cost or the other must include interest on capital, or one will have one cost price and the other another. In such a case to include interest on capital might not and probably would not absolutely equalize conditions, but it does so as far as is possible in accordance with existing facts.

In order to simply illustrate a matter like this it is necessary to take its simpler phases. But in large and complex manufacturing concerns, the variations in the relationship between interest on capital employed and other costs are not simple and obvious, but often numerous and obscure, and it follows that a uniform addition to other costs in order to provide remuneration for capital employed in production will not result in a true statement of total cost or a just basis for selling prices.

The second feature of Mr. Church's plan that it is necessary to consider carefully is the "Supplementary Rate" by which the expenses attaching to idle machines are dealt with. Mr. Church's supplementary rate includes other charges in addition to idle machine charges, but it is in relation to the latter that it is considered here. For the sake of clearness it will be well to explain first exactly how the machine rate, which runs against the machine whether it is operated or idle, is built up.

The first consideration is the cost of factory floor-space. This cost consists of interest on the investment in land and buildings, repairs and depreciation on buildings, and the expense of heating and lighting buildings. If all the factory space is of similar character, the cost of the square foot of floor-space is arrived at by dividing the total cost by the total square feet. It is, however, plain that if for some special purpose a room having additional height were necessary, there would be increased cost of providing floor-space in such a room. And if a building of one story were needed, to combine with ground-floor space, overhead light and ventilation, the investment and the expenses per square foot of floor-space in such a building would be very much increased. When the total expense of factory space is arrived at, it is not especially difficult upon careful examination to make the distinctions necessary in order to determine the cost that properly attaches to each building and to each room. Such distinctions are constantly made, and probably with great accuracy, for the purpose of fixing rents.

In the case of a machine shop the space occupied by each machine has next to be determined in order to include in the machine rate the number of square feet of floor-space occupied, at the cost per square foot. This is the first item in the machine rate.

Then follows the expenses of the machine itself. Interest on the investment in the machine, the annual repairs and depreciation charge, and other expenses which upon thorough analysis of the expense accounts are found to attach to the individual machines or to be capable of being apportioned to them. It is not necessary to go into these for the immediate purpose, and they will be dealt with fully in due course. The expense of power gives a separate rate only chargeable to the machine running.

The total of the expenses to be included in the machine rate being arrived at, it is divided by the total working hours in the year, less a reasonable deduction for minimum lost time, and the hourly rate for the machine is arrived at.

If then a machine is idle for a day or a week the expenses which attach to that machine during that idle time have to be disposed of, and Mr. Church includes them with the quite indirect and general expenses of the shop, and divides the total by the number of machine hours operated, and the rate so arrived at is added to the machine charges in the cost accounts for jobs worked upon. Mr. Church lays emphasis on the fact that the rise or fall of the supplementary rate indicates the fuller or slacker operation of the shops, and provides perhaps certain other gauges of efficiency.

It is one of the purposes of these articles to advocate a different method of dealing with the expenses of factory capacity idle.

It has been seen that the great reason for including interest on capital in the cost of products is that then, whatever the peculiarity of circumstances, the method is always adjusted to them, and costs are always stated on a single and sound basis. We need to deal with the cost of factory capacity idle by a method for which the same thing can be said.

Obviously no method can fulfill this condition that provides for charging into the cost of products the expense of factory capacity idle. The cost figure for any article depends then for one thing upon certain arbitrary divisions of time. If the distribution is made monthly an article produced in the first week of the month will have its cost increased by machinery being idle in the last week. If the distribution is semi-monthly this would not be the case. No article produced in the month would have the same cost under the monthly as under the semi-monthly distribution. This aspect of the matter would possibly not be of great importance if all goods were made for immediate sale, and consequently a cost statement were seen once for what it is and then disposed of. But in machine shops a considerable part of the manufacture is of standardized parts for the storehouse, and these go into store at their cost figures and later on are drawn out with other parts and assembled. If in the cost of each part there is the ever varying accident of the charge for machines not operated in one month or another, the final cost of an assembled article is not of a known character—it may include much or little expense for machines idle. An economy might have been effected in its production since the last time it was made, and it might yet show a higher cost. Everything of course is traceable, but in actual practice there is not time to trace everything. Moreover to trace such a difference would only be to arrive at facts that had already been known at the proper time, and cost figures should not, if it can be avoided, raise questions uselessly.

But there are other conditions under which the attempt to

take up in the cost prices of products all expenses of factory capacity idle, results in producing figures that are without significance and can only cause confusion and error. Such conditions exist, for instance, when a new producer enters the market. Factory capacity has been created and put into operation, and the competition of older concerns has to be met with the most careful judgment. The factory output is necessarily small at the very first. What is the cost of the product during that period in which operations are being gradually increased? Possibly, in one sense, it is such figures as will absorb all the factory expenses, but it will serve one's purpose just as well to know that fact in bulk as in detail, and if one has factory accounts they should show something different from this.

If the factory accounts, under such circumstances, aim to determine the proper and necessary cost of the product by separating the cost of that capacity which is as yet not used, they will give figures disentangled from the temporary and unavoidable condition of under-operation. Such figures will determine whether proper conditions have been created in the factory, and whether, subject only to selling a full output, one can manufacture at a profit or whether defects in equipment or processes need remedying.

What then is to be done under these and under any other circumstances with the expenses of factory capacity idle? What treatment of the matter will keep one's cost figures, in relation to this also, always on a single and sound basis?

If there exists in a factory a recurring loss of a certain character, not necessarily incident to the turning out of the factory product, but on the other hand an unavoidable loss, or at least a loss that will be greater or less according to the efficiency of the shop or commercial management, the best way to treat that loss in the books is to open a separate and conspicuous account for it, and it would be worth while to open such an account for the expense of "Factory Capacity Idle," even if it were proposed afterwards to absorb it into the cost of products. It is in this case not proposed to absorb it into the cost of products, but to keep the costs of the products of the factory operated and the cost of the factory idle separate from one another.

The full operation of a factory depends upon engineering and commercial efficiency, and upon efficiency of shop management.

257

11

If the cost of falling short of full operation is constantly and clearly stated, the units of idle capacity being identified and the causes traceable, there is created entirely new likelihood that effective remedies will be applied.

It is the distinguishing mark of a true method that it does not merely accomplish an immediate desired end, but that all its remoter operation is beneficial, in ways foreseen and in ways unforeseen. The abandonment of percentages making a simply inaccurate distribution of certain expenses, and the substitution of the individual machine charge, lead to the exact statement of capacity unused, and this sets at work influences tending to bring that unused capacity into operation. This it does first by relieving cost prices of a burden that does not belong to them, thereby creating immediately a better condition commercially, and next by bringing into plain view the cost of idle factory capacity, and making it possible to trace its causes and to fix responsibility for it and to secure earnest and well-directed efforts to remedy it. It will be seen when the possibilities of the organization of other departments are considered that the mere fact of there being a record of idle machines will tend to bring them into use by securing a more even distribution of work throughout shops and throughout a period of time. And finally there will be noted the effect of it all upon the steady employment of labor, in simple illustration of the principle, which we shall later on see operating in equally certain but less obvious ways, that the interests of the employer and the employed are not antagonistic, but are one.

In the succeeding articles it is proposed to deal in detail with the organization of the shop accounts and records, and with their uses.

JOHN WHITMORE.

New York.

Factory Accounting as Applied to Machine Shops.

II.

BY JOHN WHITMORE.

The organization of a factory and its system of accounts and records are so closely allied, are so inseparable, that to talk of one is necessarily to talk of the other. It may indeed be said that the system of accounts and records is the fabric of any adequate organization, the very means by which the factory methods and routine are given definite and concrete shape. Whatever in the factory methods and routine does not find expression in the accounts and records is apt to be of the nature of usage imperfectly defined and not invariably observed. If this practical identity of the factory accounts and the factory organization is borne in mind, it will be easy to realize that the factory accounting will not consist of separate and independent systems for the several departments, as a " storehouse system," a " cost department system," and so on, but of one system that must be coextensive with the whole of the operations, a system of which all the parts shall be carefully related to each other and co-ordinated to a single end. In describing such a system, it is necessary to take the features of it up one by one, and at the same time it will be found impossible to dispose of any one feature without considerable reference to others. It may even be that a really exhaustive discussion of any one feature of a perfectly developed system would be found to have included reference to every other feature of it. Relatively, however, to the possibilities of elucidation which exist in connection with the subject of the interdependence of the departments of a manufacturing business, and the consequent interdependence of all the parts of any working system applied to it, the present discussion must necessarily be rather introductory than exhaustive.

For the purpose of describing a system of factory accounts the convenient units are rather the books or other forms or means of record, than divisions of the factory or of the operations. And the most convenient starting point, as it is necessarily the finishing point, is not any one of the factory books or records, but the general ledger of the commercial accounts, because in this general ledger the whole of the factory records are synthesized and con-

345

13

trolled, it may be roughly said, in two accounts, representing respectively materials provided for the manufacturing purposes, and the manufacturing operations. These accounts may be called stores account and manufacturing account, and in connection with them it will be convenient to speak of the stock account, to which the factory product, credited to the manufacturing account, is debited. The manufacturing account is, however, a single account ultimately rather than immediately. It is convenient and it is even necessary to keep it in the first place in somewhat analyzed form by means of a number of subsidiary accounts, which are, however, parts of the manufacturing account and are finally closed into it. It is not merely convenient, but pertinent, to consider here the finished stock account in conjunction with the stores account and the manufacturing account, because the three accounts together furnish continuous control of all stocks, raw, in process, and finished, from the time of the purchase of the first to the time of the sale of the last. This control is similar to the control over cash which is obtained by means of the cash account. In the lectures referred to at the beginning of these articles this parallel between the purpose and the method of the three accounts representing stocks, and the much more familiar cash account, was dwelt upon, because it seemed that if the closeness of the parallel was seen, the idea of the three accounts must thereafter be as familiar as the idea of the cash account, and the parallel was illustrated as follows :—

General Ledger Account: Subsidiary Books:	Cash. Cash Book.	Stores. Stores Ledger.	Manufacturing. Cost Ledger.	Finished Stock. Stock Ledger.
Debits:	Checks received.	Purchase Invoices.	Stores Orders, etc.	Stock Debit. Notes.
Credits:	Checks paid.	Stores Orders.	Stock Debit Notes.	Merchandise Orders.

There is a difference in the case of the manufacturing account, indicated by the " et cetera " because that account is not debited and credited with goods in the same state, and is consequently further debited with all the expense of converting them from one state to another. But throughout this process of conversion from one state to another the accounting control can be made as continuous and effective as that which is exercised in the other cases by means of the other accounts. This is obviously not accomplished by merely keeping a manufacturing account and a cost ledger, but it is accomplished in the full development of the factory accounting. And in the lectures referred to another distinction was noted for the purpose of bringing out what must be the central idea in factory organization. The distinction is that cash, and stores, and finished stock, are drawn upon as requirements outside of themselves arise, and that the department represented by the manufacturing account delivers its goods when it is itself ready to do so; which may be taken as typical of the fact that because in the final developments of the business every requirement is made of the producing departments, therefore all the organization is directed to giving the producing departments the utmost facilities in all their working, and in delivering to them everything they need, and in receiving from them when they are ready to deliver. Obviously then one of the vital purposes to be accomplished in the factory organization is to enable the storehouse to supply the needs of the producing departments, or shops, without any delay that can possibly be guarded against. To this end the engineering department, the purchasing department, and the storehouse itself, must contribute by the most systematic and co-ordinated working, and the accounting instrument by which alone the desired result can be accomplished is the stores ledger. It is scarcely necessary to add that for the purpose in view the stores ledger is elaborated beyond the mere provision for debiting goods received and crediting goods issued. Here is a stores ledger form designed to include every precaution against delays in filling the shop requisitions. *(See form on next page.)*

The control of the storehouse is exercised through the engineering department because the engineering department alone possesses all the qualifications for exercising such control wisely and to every good result. It possesses the best knowledge of the qualities of materials, the best knowledge of the hazards of breakdowns and the consequent needs of stocks for repairs, the best knowledge of impending or probable changes in the design or construction of machines, and the best opportunities to adjust designs at times so as to bring into use materials that might otherwise become inactive. Taking the ordinary case of a business making and selling standard and special machines, two kinds of information are necessary in order that the supplies in a storehouse shall be kept adjusted to the shop requirements. The first relates to the general volume and character of the business, and

347

15

Article ————

Stock Limit ————

Standard Order ————

RECEIVED							DELIVERED						WANTED				ORDERED		
Date	Inv. No.	From	Order No.	Quan.	Price	Am't	Date	Stores Order	Shop Order	Quan.	Price	Am't	List of Materials		Stores Orders		Req'n	Order	Quan.
													Shop Order	Quan.	Shop Order	Quan.			

348

16

the second to the actual contracts made by the selling department. The first concerns materials of various characters and for various purposes. New machine parts which are standard either because of a practically invariable character for their particular uses or because of special standardization making these parts uniform in machines that may otherwise vary, are made more conveniently and cheaply in quantities for stock, and if the quantities are carefully judged a minimum cost is obtained with little risk of an offsetting loss through any part of such stock becoming inactive. Then with a given quantity of the product of the shops sold and in use and subject to wear and tear, there will have come into existence certain current needs of parts for repair purposes. Again there are supplies of standard materials in their first state, that is, as they are purchased, each having a certain average consumption established. For all these classes of storehouse materials, and for all ordinary machine shop supplies whether purchased or manufactured for store, the general conditions of the business furnish guidance in the maintenance of stocks, and the resulting decisions and instructions are expressed in stock limits, the quantities below which the stocks must not fall, and standard orders, being the standard quantities to requisition when the stock limits are reached, and these stock limits and standard orders are fixed by the engineering department, and it is the duty of the storehouse to continually scrutinize them in the light of its records and to ask for revision in every case where it seems necessary.

The soundness of the figures of the stock limits and standard orders is a matter of very great importance, and it can only be attained by perfecting the influence of the engineering department over the storehouse, and by establishing the closest touch between them. In large businesses with a product of complex or varied character, and consequently with operations and stocks requiring the most careful and systematic control, it is advisable for the engineering department to have a card index corresponding to the titles of the accounts in the storehouse ledgers and marked with the stock limit and standard order figures, so that as the engineering department develops new plans, or notes new tendencies in the sales contracts, they can, with facility, inform themselves exactly concerning stocks of materials carried under existing instructions and give new instructions without waiting for a disparity between stocks and shop needs to become evident in the

349

17

storehouse. For two reasons especially the highest efficiency of the factory organization as it relates to the storehouse department is of vital importance. The first is that the economical operation of the shops depends for one thing upon the storehouse filling all stores orders immediately they are presented. The second is that the requisitions it must issue are the basis of large expenditures. The stock limits and standard orders, if they are made to express the latest knowledge and the most careful judgment of the engineering department and are continually criticised in the light of the experience of actual consumption recorded in the stores ledgers, are an important safeguard in relation to both these matters. The next precaution is that all storehouse requisitions shall go through the engineering department for approval before they are effective in the purchasing department, or as a basis for shop orders to produce for the storehouse. This gives the control of the engineering department over the storehouse the twofold operation that efficient control must have, first through the freedom to exercise itself at such times and in such places as current conditions in its judgment call for, and second through a routine that brings the things done or proposed to be done, systematically under review. The precautions in regard to expenditures under storehouse requisitions are not completed by the engineering department approval. Well understood responsibilities for expenditure rest upon the purchasing department, which must call attention to any commercial conditions on account of which requisitions should in its opinion be modified.

Having provided for the maintenance of stocks in accordance with the general character and volume of the business, the next thing is to make particular provision for actual sales contracts, and it is to serve this purpose that the next special features of the stores ledger form are provided. If finished apparatus is to be manufactured for stock, the decision to manufacture is, as far as the storehouse and shops are concerned, exactly equivalent to sales contracts for such apparatus, as they will be delivered to the finished stock department exactly as they would in the other case be delivered to the shipping department, and are quite probably manufactured in anticipation that they may be sold by the time the shops can finish them. If the storehouse is to foresee and provide for the shop needs, it is plain that it must be promptly advised of all undertakings to build and deliver the machines which are the shop product. Lists of the materials entering into standard machines should be in the possession of the storehouse, so that when the storehouse is advised what standard machines it has been contracted to produce, it knows what materials the shop will sooner or later call for in respect of such contracts. In the case of machines which are not standard machines there are special designs, and drawings, and lists of materials, and these special lists of materials have to be furnished to the storehouse with the advice of such a contract. This is to say, the storehouse is advised as soon as possible of all machines that the shops have got to produce, and the storehouse either has or is furnished with information concerning everything which enters into those machines, and which the shops will in due time call upon the storehouse to furnish to them. Undertakings to build machines, whether for sales contracts or for stock, should immediately be given a shop order number, and this number is a part of the advice sent to the storehouse. The lists of materials are then posted to the stores ledger accounts under the general heading " Wanted " and the sub-heading " Lists of Materials—Shop Order—Quantity." This entry affects the relation of the actual stock to the stock limit inasmuch as certain materials are thereby practically assigned to a certain shop order and no longer form part of the free balance. This may or may not result in the issue of a requisition. If it does, an entry of the date and quantity is made under the general heading " Ordered " and the sub-heading " Requisition."

It may, of course, happen, in spite of the best efforts that stores orders will yet be presented for some of these materials before the storehouse is ready to deliver them. In such a case the stores order is entered under the general heading " Wanted " and sub-heading " Stores Orders—Shop Order—Quantity." The shop order number identifies the want as the same one previously entered, but neither entry is superfluous. The first one may, either immediately or later, have shown the necessity of issuing a requisition, and the second makes the important record that the shops are actually waiting for the materials, and immediately they are received the clerk entering the debit advises the proper person that such stores orders can now be filled. Such proper person is, of course, whoever in the storehouse has charge of unfilled stores orders. The provision for entering under " Delivered " the shop order number for which the delivery is made, is to enable one to see whether stores orders entered under the heading " Wanted " have subsequently been filled. So the actual stocks and all known wants, standard, immediate, and future, are recorded. It remains to complete the record as to incoming supplies. Mention has been made of the entry in the stores ledger account of requisitions issued. Such requisitions may be the basis of orders issued by the purchasing department, or of orders to the shops to manufacture for the storehouse. It is not sufficient for the storehouse to know that it has issued a requisition. It needs to know always whether the deliveries on it are complete, and for this purpose it is convenient to know the number of the purchase or shop order issued. Moreover the latter may not always be exactly in accordance with the requisition. This part of the storehouse record is put on a sound basis if the storehouse is either given access to records of both purchase orders and shop orders for storehouse, or is furnished with a carbon copy of these orders, entering then this order number under the general heading " Ordered " and the sub-heading " Order—Quantity." Then every invoice of materials purchased and every debit note for goods made by the shops for the storehouse should bear the number of purchase order or shop order, and this number is part of the posting to the debit side of the stores ledger account. Now the stores ledger account shows not only the actual stock, and all known wants, but also the exact condition of outstanding requisitions and purchase or shop orders. Of course, under the heading " Ordered " far from every line is used, and so, without providing more columns, there is plenty of room to note anything of importance, especially date when delivery is promised or expected. Careful watch should be kept by the stores ledger keepers for overdue materials, and a regular form used to request the purchasing department to trace. It is a natural question how much clerical help it takes to effectively maintain such records. One answer is impossible, for only experience can in any given case show. But some pertinent considerations are worth dwelling upon.

First, experience will in any given case show, because the work is visible. It is the work of clerks manifestly engaged in doing it. It is not the irregular work of a lot of worried people in various departments, needing to know continually about materials for different purposes, and making inquiries and search in various quarters, and then perhaps failing to get accurate information.

The systematic record increases the visible labor in connection with the materials item, but it is not equally certain that it increases the actual labor, or the immediate expense of it. Beyond the immediate expense there is the result. To perfectly supply the shop needs without carrying excessive stocks of materials is a condition to be striven for and never perfectly attained. Every step by which one comes nearer to it is a step nearer to the full utilization of the shop capacity, and makes simpler all the broad problems of shop and business management. To sacrifice even a very little here to save a good deal of clerical work is a doubtful economy, and that the sacrifice in the shop working is small and the offsetting economy large are two things it is very difficult to be sure of. There remain to be noted other ways in which the storehouse organization and records can be made helpful in securing final economy in production, and then there remain to be described the methods by which agreement between the general ledger stores account and the stores ledgers, and the actual stocks in the storehouse, is maintained. Finally there will be noted the facilities furnished by the accounts and records for the control of the general management over all the departments concerned.

The rule that the storehouse issues requisitions for materials as stocks reach or approach the stock limit fixed by the engineering department may be given a little elasticity. There are groups of materials that it is advantageous to order together whether they are to be purchased or to be produced in the shops. It is desirable that as occasion arises to order a stock of one of the articles in such a group, reference to the accounts for the other articles in the same group shall be easily made, to see whether some of these are also at a point justifying the placing of an order. This is one consideration that should influence the sequence of the accounts in the stores ledgers. Reference may here be made to another possible use of the stores ledgers with their fullness of record. Some systematic index might be made of stock articles produced on the different machines respectively, so that in the case of a certain plant being idle it might be promptly and definitely and exhaustively ascertained whether any stock articles the production of which would employ such idle plant were at a point at which reordering for stock would, under the circumstances, be justified. If it is thought that there might be a dangerous tendency in this, it must be remembered that such reordering would be accomplished by means of a storehouse requisition approved by the engineering department, which is a very different thing from letting the shops decide to make a good showing at the risk of overproduction. The storehouse receives goods from concerns bought from, and from the shops. In the former case it has purchase invoices, in the latter stores debit notes. After certifying the receipt of the goods on these documents postings are made from them to the stores ledger accounts, and such postings are plainly signified on the documents. The latter is important, as this posting-mark should always be seen at the time the purchase invoices or stores debit notes are entered in journal or summary sheet, from which the monthly posting of totals is made to the stores account in the general ledger. By these means any omission to post a debit to a stores ledger account will be detected. Each department of the shops that may receive from and deliver to the storehouse has its own series of stores orders and its own series of stores debit notes. The storehouse neither delivers to the shops nor receives from them except by means of one of these. Each series of stores orders and each series of stores debit notes is consecutively numbered by the printer. Stores debit notes are entered in the stores ledger accounts immediately they and the goods represented by them are received in the storehouse, but this entry is necessarily without price and extension. They are then sent to the cost clerks, who price and extend and post in the cost ledgers, and return to the storehouse for completion of the postings there.

A monthly summary sheet is kept for each series of stores orders and each series of stores debit notes, and on each summary sheet the original numerical order is retained, to show if any documents are unaccounted for. Stores orders which have been presented, and which the storehouse has not been able to fill on presentation, and which go over the end of a month unfilled, will naturally be missing numbers in the monthly summary sheet and must go over to the next month's sheet. An important test of efficiency in the storehouse is its ability to fill the stores orders promptly, and here is a simple means of seeing each month how many orders are, at a given point of time, waiting to be filled. If the management will take these up each month and learn why the delays have occurred, another strong influence will be at work to secure the important end that the productive operations shall be facilitated to the fullest extent by the storehouse furnishing materials as they are needed.

Now there is made possible a new method in place of the old periodical inventory takings. Stocks of materials are now managed by means of the stores ledger records, and it is very important that there should be no doubt of the accuracy of these records. When a stores ledger account shows the stock of a certain material low, an additional safeguard is created if, before ordering more, the actual stock is counted and the ledger figure verified. The ledger balance being verified, it is brought down in the account as a verified balance, and this goes on from day to day throughout the year. The inventory as stated in the stores ledgers is always in process of verification, and the work of verification is reduced to a minimum by taking each stock when it is at its lowest point, and the work is spread out pretty evenly through the year, instead of the whole thing being attempted as at a single date, usually with great inconvenience, and usually with inaccurate results. Of course actual counts do not always agree exactly with ledger figures, and then an adjustment is necessary. It is well to provide the storehouse with its own series of stores debit and credit notes, by means of which adjustments of either quantities or valuations may be recorded. The necessity to adjust valuations arises when any stores are found to be inactive and consequently of decreased value, a matter that has to be dealt with especially at balance sheet dates. These debit and credit notes must be summarized on a monthly sheet, from which the entry in the general ledger stores account and the corresponding entry in the general ledger stores adjustment account will be posted. It would indeed be well to keep two stores adjustment accounts in the general ledger, one for adjustments in respect of quantities and one for adjustments in respect of values, for the adjustments in respect of quantities are a test of the efficiency of the control exercised by the storehouse over the stocks of materials in its charge, and the adjustments in respect of values are a test of the judgment and care with which the engineering department guards against inactive stocks.

If storehouse accounts kept in the fashion described are audited at the close of a year, the auditors can see when each account was last verified, and they can call for the verification of

355

23

accounts with stocks where it seems desirable to do so, either because the value represented is large, or because the latest verification is of too remote a date. They can draw off a statement from the ledgers of all inactive items and ascertain their total, and enquire in detail concerning their valuation. They have means of judging of the accuracy and soundness, from all points of view, of the inventory statement furnished by the ledgers, and they come into a position where they can certify to its practical accuracy, or point out clearly the weaknesses in the records which need to be remedied. Later on it will be seen how the cost ledgers furnish an inventory of everything in process as excellent, both as to simplicity and as to accuracy, as the materials inventory furnished by the stores ledgers. The auditor's list of inactive materials should be used to the fullest possible extent for the purpose of moving such materials, that is to say, the list must go to every department that may be able to contribute directly or indirectly to this end, especially the engineering department, the sales department, and the management. In all factory accounting it is necessary to adhere to principles and to keep one's methods flexible. One must be prepared always to adjust methods of recording so that these methods will follow the proper and necessary course of the operations. It has been described how in order to obtain materials from the storehouse the shops make out stores orders, and how these being filled are priced and extended and entered in the stores ledgers. There are, however, instances in which it is not convenient or economical to separate the exact quantity of material required, even if the exact quantity were known. In such cases materials may be issued on a memorandum, which is priced and extended and posted in the stores ledgers to the credit of the material accounts and to the debit of a special account opened for the temporary purpose. Such materials are afterwards accounted for by a stores order for what has been used, and the return to store of the unused balance.

A question commonly arises as to how, under certain circumstances, issues of materials ought to be priced. The stock of any material at any time may consist of two or more purchases. Sometimes the several purchases are at rather widely differing prices. Even if the article is one that is produced in the shops the successive cost figures may not be the same. It is probably the best rule that, whatever the conditions, issues of materials are best priced at the average cost of the existing stock, that is, the money balance of the account divided by the quantity balance. This figure once determined is in force until a new purchase, or production, is made at a cost different from the average figure being used, and to any methods described here or anywhere else there must be added whatever experience suggests as calculated to contribute to the end that stocks of materials shall be such active necessary stocks as will promptly meet all shop needs.*

* Erratum : In the August number of THE JOURNAL, page 257, twelfth line from bottom, for "unavoidable," read "avoidable."

Factory Accounting as Applied to Machine Shops.

III.

By John Whitmore.

Absolutely all of the work of determining the cost of manufacture ought to be effective also for the purpose of controlling the cost. This applies of course to cost accounting and not at all to cost estimating. One may know exactly what materials ought to be used to produce certain finished goods, and on the basis of such knowledge costs may be estimated, but this does nothing to insure the proper consumption of materials, and so far no provision is made to detect excessive consumption. The same remarks apply to labor and to all other expenses of production.

But if materials are controlled in a storehouse and can only be obtained thence by means of orders which are used in the accounting to credit the storehouse and to debit the individual cost account, then a record of the consumption, whatever it may be, is created, and there come into existence the means of seeing whether things are right or wrong and of applying any necessary correction. The same is true of a completely distributed productive labor pay-roll.

The danger and the expense of wasted materials and wasted labor are known and borne in mind by all careful manufacturers, and the importance of safeguards against such waste is pretty generally appreciated. It may be repeated that such safeguards are created by means of accounting and not of estimating. The exact record is the only means of accurate knowledge, and accurate knowledge the only basis for systematic correction and improvement.

All this is to be borne in mind when we come to the accounting for factory capacity. If there is any difference it is that the conditions which exist in relation to the economical utilization of materials and labor, are intensified in relation to the economical utilization of factory capacity, for the reason that in regard to the last, standards of economy are less simple, less generally appreciated; and less strictly enforced.

Between the means ordinarily used in business management

430

and in cost accounts to watch the utilization of factory capacity and to deal with its cost, and a strict accounting for factory capacity, there is the same distinction that exists between estimates and strict accounts for materials and labor, that is, the strict accounting furnishes means of control which the other does not. It is worth while to be absolutely clear about this, and therefore to stop to consider what the means ordinarily used are.

In the first place, of course every factory manager knows that he needs a certain volume of work. The sales department exists to secure contracts which will keep the factory busy. If the factory equipment and products are of a simple character this insistence on volume of business together with vigilant supervision of the factory may pretty nearly meet the necessities of the case so far as utilization of factory capacity goes. It is doubtful whether it ever quite does so, unless in the case of continuous processes to make a uniform product. In machine shops some machines may be overcrowded and others idle, and much more than mere volume of business is needed to secure full utilization of the shop capacity.

Again the ordinary means of representing the cost of factory capacity in the cost accounts for the products are undoubtedly the ascertaining of the charges for factory capacity, and often for many other expenses together therewith, in a year's accounts, and the ascertaining of the ratio between the total of these and the productive labor charge, and thereafter the adding of the apparently necessary percentage to the productive labor item. If the factory is of a very simple character, and if the year's accounts from which the percentage is derived represent average full operation of the factory, something like accurate costs may be arrived at by these means. This is not saying much, as any degree of simplicity in operations and records may be supposed. Obviously no such simplicity exists in machine shop operations. The assumption in such a method is that factory equipment and labor are always utilized equally. Nothing could be further from the case in machine shops. Often expensive labor is used with slight use of machinery or small tools, and again the most expensive machinery is used with relatively little labor. Plainly in the case of machine shops the means ordinarily used for obtaining the full utilization of factory capacity and for determining the cost of the respective products are not calculated to really

431

27

accomplish either one or the other. They are in fact in some respects much weaker in comparison with an actual accounting for factory capacity, than estimates of materials and labor in relation to an actual accounting for the same, inasmuch as these estimates may represent what ought to be the facts, while a uniform percentage added to productive labor in machine shop cost accounts either has for its basis conditions which no longer exist, or is from first to last merely a makeshift.

It is worth while to consider carefully why the matter of accounting strictly for the use of factory capacity has not generally appealed to manufacturers as of equal importance with the accounting for materials and for productive labor. All manufacturers know that the cost of factory capacity, at least in the shape of repair and depreciation charges and taxes and insurance, enters into the cost of production as truly as does the cost of materials and the cost of labor. It is the total cost and not the details of the cost that is ultimately of importance. A dollar saved in the charge for plant employed is equal to a dollar saved in the materials used. The accounting for factory capacity is perhaps a matter of rather greater difficulty; the means of doing it are less understood. This may partly explain a lesser apparent interest in doing it. But it does not fully account for the average attitude toward the matter.

It seems probable that the average feeling is that the expenditures for materials and labor are current expenditures which are greater or less from day to day according as there is greater or less economy or waste, while the existence of the plant and the necessity of maintaining it are fixed facts entailing a practically fixed expenditure. By taking thought to-morrow's expenditure for materials or labor may be more or less, but not the expenditure which enters into the cost of the factory product as plant charges. If this is true it means that waste impresses the average man more or less according as its effect upon the cash account is immediate or remote, and that upon the same principle the outgoing dollar impresses him more than the incoming one. For to increase output so that a dollar of plant charges can be taken out of the cost of the former output as being a part of the cost of the new additional output which will be sold and paid for at least at its cost, is as profitable an operation as to reduce by a dollar the cost of materials or labor.

Or it is possible that the average feeling is that a return will be obtained for the plant expense as far as the product of the factory can be sold, and that as there is no other means of obtaining a return for it it is idle to count it up as if it were remaining cash. If this is the feeling it fails to take into account influences which have their effect upon human effort: the sense of opportunity, the sense of necessity, the exact knowledge of what ought to be done. It is for one thing to set at work these influences, to show exactly what factory capacity is unutilized and what the resulting loss is, that the accounting for·factory capacity is set up.

Even the feeling that plant expense, including interest on the investment in plant, is less actual expenditure than the expense of materials and labor, or that it calls for less care in tracing it to its results, comes generally speaking from an inadequate view of things. Expenditure for plant is not made once for all time, nor is plant usually created to be worn out and to pass out of existence. The ordinary business condition is that investment in plant is continually being returned and being reinvested in plant. The investment which was made in the first place on a calculation of certain operation under certain future conditions is continually re-made with what ought to be an exact knowledge of actual operation under conditions actually existing. If an investment in plant is contemplated, one calculates whether in operation it will be profitable to the extent of paying all current expenses and a fair return upon capital. It is upon such a calculation that one creates a factory or buys a single machine. In actual operation one has the opportunity to compare alternative processes with varying machine and labor costs, and to learn not only whether a machine can be operated profitably, but whether by means of it the lowest costs of which one knows are obtained. And this knowledge should be the result of comparing cost figures which sum up all the facts, including the fact of the larger or smaller investment which the different processes necessitate.

If one can reduce the labor cost of production by increasing the machine cost, and vice versa, it follows that to compare labor costs only might lead to conclusions that would be modified and possibly reversed upon comparison of combined machine and labor costs. And if processes having higher costs are to be systematically eliminated in favor of those having lower costs, it is the complete cost of each that must be known and available for quick use. And if plant expenses are actual costs, as materials and labor are actual costs, they must be included in cost accounts according to actually determined facts, and not by an arbitrary or makeshift distribution creating the appearance of profits or losses which are not actual, and furnishing an unsound basis for the selling operations.

For these reasons it is necessary to arrive as closely as possible at the hourly expense of each machine and to record machine time as accurately as a workman's time is recorded, and to charge the machine expense for the job into the cost account for the job, exactly as the labor expense is charged.

The hourly expense of each machine is made up of the expense of land and buildings and of the machine itself. The expense of land and buildings is first distributed to the several divisions of the plant that have to be dealt with separately in the cost accounts. What these divisions are depends upon the individual situation. Necessarily there is the storehouse with its own expense account, and the tool room with its own expense account, and various offices. Space not occupied by machines but used for assembling is dealt with separately. The space occupied by the power plant, the expenses of the power machinery, and all other expenses of power, are dealt with in a group, and are brought into the cost accounts by means of a charge per horse power hour for machines running. It is necessary to have a rate per hour for each machine chargeable in the cost account for the whole time the machine is engaged upon the job, including the time occupied in setting up the machine, in putting materials into it, and taking materials out of it, up to the time it is released ready for the next job. The power time, being the actual running time of the machine, is necessarily less than the machine time, so that the machine rate is chargeable for a certain number of hours and the power rate for a lesser number. The whole subject of the accounting for power expense, perhaps the most difficult problem in machine shop cost accounts, must be taken up by itself.

The first item in the machine rate is then the charge for factory space, the most convenient unit of which is the square foot of floor-space. This charge consists of the following items: 1. Interest on the cost of land; 2. Interest on the cost of buildings; 3. Expense of repairing buildings; 4. Charge for depreciation of buildings; 5. Expense of heating and lighting buildings; 6. Insurance and taxes on land and buildings. The term buildings is here used as including certain working equipment, such as heating and lighting fixtures, elevators, wash-rooms, etc. These however should not be included with buildings in a single general ledger account, for they are as a rule subject to a higher rate of depreciation.

While buildings do not actually cover the land on which they stand, the floor-space in the buildings is chargeable with the whole expense of the land, unless some of the land is either unused or used for some purpose the expense of which is dealt with separately from the floor-space charge. Thus yard-space used for storage purposes is chargeable to storehouse expense, and not to the cost of factory floor-space. On the other hand, the yard-space which is necessary for purposes of light, and in order to handle work conveniently between the several shops, is properly treated as a part of the expense of factory floor-space.

When the total cost of floor-space has been ascertained, and the floor-space itself has been measured and the measurement of each separate room recorded, the total cost is divided by the total measurement, and the cost of the square foot of floor-space is arrived at. Then there is distributed to each room its proportionate cost, which in the case of machine shops fully occupied by machines is afterwards absorbed in the machine rates. Not all floor-space however is used for machines, or for directly productive operations. There is the storehouse space already alluded to, and there may be other space reserved for the storage of large castings in machine shops. All of this is charged to storehouse expense exactly as was the cost of yard-space used for storage purposes. And floor-space is needed for both factory and general offices, and the charges for these are added to the general factory expenses and the general office expenses respectively.

The next step is to measure the space taken by the individual machines. The manner of determining these measurements should always be carefully considered. Perhaps the best rule is to arrive at a four-sided rectangular space which will just suffice to accommodate the machine in operation, unless it is plain that this would include space which is either constantly or occasionally put to other uses. The total space in the shop, less the total space measured as occupied by machines, is the working

435

space which is to be regarded as existing for the benefit of the machines impartially, unless upon examination some distinction is recognized. If there is no such distinction then the space measured for each machine is to be increased by such a percentage as will complete the distribution of the shop space to machines. The machine space thus arrived at, at the cost per square foot already determined, is the first item in the expense of the machine for the year.

The next thing to take into consideration in determining a machine rate is the present value of the machine and its estimated remaining years of life. Upon these the interest and depreciation charges are based. An equitable charge for depreciation will probably be made if a rate is used which, written off the decreasing balances from year to year, will reduce a machine to ten per cent. of its cost by the end of its estimated lifetime. This gives the highest charge when a machine is new and presumably at its highest efficiency, both actual and relative, and a steadily decreasing charge from year to year.

Next there is the matter of the annual repair charge. Shop foremen can tell pretty well what the bare expense of maintaining a machine in working order is, exclusive of accidents. When such a figure is stated it may be doubled to cover repairs from all causes, in order to arrive at a roughly fair figure to use until actual records correct it. An actual record of the cost of repairing each machine should be kept in a machinery ledger. The machinery ledger contains an account for each machine, its number, and description, and location in the shops, and its value. Depreciation is written off each account from year to year, and the ledger is always kept in agreement with the machinery account in the general ledger. If machines are disposed of, the difference between book valuation and selling price or scrap value is known and the accounts are easily and accurately adjusted. Columns should be provided for the record of repairs: date, shop order number, and amount. As all records of repairs to machines, whether labor or material records, bear the number of the machine repaired, postings to the machine ledger accounts are easily made, and a continuous record of the cost of repairing each machine is created.

If power is transmitted by means of shafting, belting, and pulleys, we have to take into consideration the interest on the investment in the equipment, and the expense of keeping it in repair, and a fair depreciation charge. The average horse power taken by each machine when in operation is calculated as closely as it is possible to do this, and the sum of these figures, being the average horse power taken by all the machines in operation, is arrived at. The expense of interest, repairs, and depreciation, upon shafting, belting, and pulleys, is divided by this total horse power to determine what charge in each machine rate, per unit of power required to operate, will take up this expense. If all the machines in operation would, to use mere round figures throughout, take 100 horse power available at the machines, that is exclusive of power lost in transmission, and if the total expense attaching to the transmission equipment were $1,000 per annum, and if a certain machine is calculated to use on an average two horse power when in operation, the resulting charge in the yearly expense for that machine is $20.

The next expense that has to be dealt with is the expense of cranes. The process of figuring this expense is very similar to the process of figuring the expense of a machine tool. There may or may not be a floor-space charge. There is always interest on the investment in the crane and the expenses of repairs and depreciation. Then there is an estimate, and necessarily it is an estimate only, of the power used by the crane. A shop foreman knowing the average use of a crane and an engineer able to make an approximate calculation of the power used in given operations, should together be able to make a fairly close estimate. The total horse power hours so estimated, at the ascertained cost per horse power hour, is then brought into the yearly expense of the crane, and this yearly expense of the crane is then apportioned between the machine tools served by the crane, and this is the item of crane service which enters into the hourly rate for the machine.

There are other items which properly enter into the annual expense of the individual machine tool. The general ledger account for the sundry supplies of a machine shop department should be carefully examined to ascertain which, if any, of these supplies are used for the operation of certain machines, and in as far as supplies are for the use of certain machines and not for the purely general use of the department, the expense of them should be brought into the machine rates and not left in the department general expenses. It is to be borne in mind that the more ex-

437

penses can be brought into the individual machine expense accounts, the more exact and the more simple the cost accounts will be.

The wages of a foreman whose supervision is restricted to a limited number of machines, and is not general to the department, are also most accurately distributed by including these wages in the expense of such machines, and ultimately in the hourly rate charged for their use.

It is also desirable to bring the expenses of tools whose use is restricted to certain machines into the annual expense and the hourly rate for such machines. This can be done where the tool department and its records are systematically organized.

The items therefore which possibly enter into the hourly rate chargeable for the use of a machine are the following:

1. Floor space.
2. Interest on investment in machine.
3. Repairs to machine.
4. Depreciation of machine.
5. Proportion of shafting, belting, and pulleys expense, consisting of interest on the investment, and repairs, and depreciation.
6. Crane service.
7. Supplies which are special to the machine.
8. Proportion of superintendence which is special to a limited number of machines.
9. The expense of interest, repairs, and depreciation on tools whose use is confined to the machine.

When the annual expense of each machine has been determined, it still remains to deduce the hourly rate, and this is rather far from being a mere arithmetical calculation.

In the first place it is necessary to divide the machines into at least two classes, and for most machine shops that have been in operation for some time, into three classes. The first class will consist of machines of full efficiency, whose use is general, and whose full capacity should under proper conditions be constantly used. The second class will consist of machines of full efficiency, installed for special and occasional use, and not upon a calculation of continuous operation. The third class is for machines which are not of the highest efficiency, but which are maintained and used when other machines which could do the work more economically are busy.

438

Concerning the first class the only question is what in a reasonable view of the matter constitutes full operation. Machines are sometimes idle for repairs, and under the best conditions time is occasionally lost from other causes. If 300 days in the year are multiplied by the working hours per day and then ten per cent. deducted, and the resulting number of hours adopted as the standard of full operation for the year, such a standard would seem reasonable and certainly not too high. If the working day is 9 hours, then $300 \times 9 = 2,700$ less $10\% = 2,430$, and the annual expense of the machine is divided by 2,430, and this gives the hourly rate.

Concerning machines in the second class, inquiry must be made as to the special uses for which they have been installed, and the extent of the use calculated upon and regarded as justifying the installation, and if for instance this was 50 per cent. of the full time, the number of hours into which the yearly expense is to be divided would under the conditions above suggested be 1,215 instead of 2,430. Such a calculation as this is subject to adjustment if it is found possible to utilize the machines more fully. If the use falls below the original calculation, the deficiency must probably be regarded as capacity idle which should be operated, and the cost of it charged to idle capacity account.

For machines in the third class, i. e., machines that have not a high efficiency, which in other words are semi-obsolete, but which it is occasionally convenient to use, the hourly rate should be determined exactly as for machines in the first class, i. e., the total annual expense divided by 2,430, and this for two reasons: 1st, their use is certainly worth no more than the hourly rate so determined, and probably even on this basis the work is expensively done; and 2d, the actual cost of keeping such machines in the shops cannot be too plainly shown.

The hourly rate for each machine in the shops having been arrived at, their use in cost accounts and general books is as simple as any familiar bookkeeping work, as simple for instance as to record and distribute the productive labor pay-roll. The two records of productive labor and machine time run at first together. The labor tickets which the machinists fill out for each job worked on, state the shop order number, and the operation, and the machinists' time, and the number of the machine tool, and all this information is transcribed on the workman's individual weekly

439

sheet which is necessarily prepared for the purposes of the pay-roll. Then there is a book called a machine rates ledger, containing an account for each machine tool in the shops, and from the workmen's weekly sheets there is posted to the accounts in the machine rates ledger every item of machine time, and these items are priced and extended at the hourly rate for the machine and are thence posted to the cost ledger accounts. The charges of machine time having been posted to the machine rates ledger for a given period, which it is convenient to make even weeks instead of the month inasmuch as the postings are made from weekly sheets, a statement is drawn off from this ledger showing all the machine numbers and against each the time charged in the period and the amount of the charges. On the statement the idle time is entered and extended at the machine rate per hour. The idle time for each machine is of course the difference between the time charged in the cost accounts for actual use of the machine, and for a four weeks' period, four fifty-second parts of the number of hours into which the machine expense for the year was divided.

The completed statement, except that we are not now considering the power charge which presently will be incorporated in the machine rates ledger and in this statement, is like this:

Machine No.	Time Charged	Amount.	Idle Time.	Amount.

and the journal entry for the general books is made like this:

Manufacturing Account
Idle Capacity Account
To Machins Rates

the debit to manufacturing account being the machine time recorded on the workmen's tickets, and transcribed to their weekly sheets, and posted to machine rates ledger and cost ledger; and the debit to idle capacity account being the difference between the time so charged and the time calculated upon as full operation; and the credit to machine rates account being the full machine rates, or in other words, the full machine expense for the period.

Each account in the machine rates ledger is continuous and without entries for idle time, so that at any time a statement can be drawn off from the ledger showing the idle time of each machine from the beginning of the fiscal period to date and the cost of the idle time in each case, just as the monthly statement gives the same information for the month. The unused capacity of the shops is thus exactly stated, and its causes and the remedy can be investigated.

It may and doubtless will happen that machines are at times operated more than the hours calculated upon, and that consequently instead of debits there will in some periods and in respect of some machines be credits to the idle capacity account. Under these or any circumstances the plan laid down is to be followed, and as it is followed will be found to operate to further useful ends, and will not disclose any unsoundness.

Errata: Last month, page 353, line 5 from bottom, " in the case of a certain plant " should be " in the case of certain plant." Page 357, line 5 from top, " used, and " should be " used. And." Through a misunderstanding last month's article was not paragraphed as written. The paragraphing of the printed article may therefore be disregarded.

Factory Accounting as Applied to Machine Shops.*

IV.

By John Whitmore.

I described to you last week the way in which the cost of having and maintaining factory capacity is divided up so as to determine the cost of having and maintaining each unit of the factory capacity, that is, as far as machine-tool units are concerned. And I described to you how the factory capacity, actually utilized in making the various products of the factory, is charged into the respective cost accounts for the various products. You will remember that the method of doing this is to divide the total annual expense of a machine by the number of hours during which, according to a careful calculation, the machine should be actually used in the course of a year, thus arriving at the expense of the machine per hour; and then to record the time the machine is engaged on the individual job, or article being produced; and finally to multiply the hourly rate by the time and to charge the resulting figure into the cost account for that job, or article; and by means of the monthly summary drawn out from the machine rates ledger, to charge that same figure into the manufacturing account in the general ledger, for, as must constantly be borne in mind, the manufacturing account in the general ledger is always kept in agreement with the sum of the open cost accounts.

And you will remember that I said to you that inasmuch as machines may be idle, not only for that small proportion of their time which under the best management may be unavoidable, but also from lack of business, or from faults in the shop management, or because machines are ill adapted to the work of the shop; and inasmuch as the expense of machines when they are idle from these latter causes is no part of the proper and necessary cost of the article produced by the machines in operation; therefore this expense of machines idle is not, either with the greatest propriety, or with the greatest convenience or usefulness, charged into the cost of the articles produced, but is charged to a separate account for idle capacity. This completes the disposition of the expenses which were absorbed in the machine rates.

You will further remember that for these debits to the manu-

*Note: This article is a reproduction, without change, of the fourth of the lectures up on which the present series of articles is based.

20

facturing account in the general ledger and to the idle capacity account in the general ledger, the corresponding credit is made to a general ledger account entitled " Machine Rates Account."

Now the expenses which have been absorbed into the machine rates are, first, a proportion of the following representing the cost of factory space:

Interest on investment in land.

Interest on investment in buildings.

Repairs to buildings.

Depreciation of buildings.

Heat and light.

Taxes on land and buildings.

Insurance on buildings.

Second, the whole of the following representing the cost of machinery:

Interest on investment in machinery.

Repairs to machinery.

Depreciation of machinery.

Taxes on machinery.

Insurance on machinery.

And I described to you last week how the machine rates might also include expenses which would be represented in the general ledger by three additional accounts, viz.:

Special supplies.

Special superintendence.

Special tools expense.

I told you last week that the cost of factory space is distributed at least to the following:

Cost of power.

Machine rates.

Storehouse expense.

General factory expense.

General office expense.

The charges for factory space to the general ledger accounts representing these expenses should be made monthly, a fixed monthly charge to each according to the floor-space ascertained to be taken by each, at the cost per square foot of floor-space determined as I described to you last week. When these debits are made, a corresponding credit has to be made, and for this pur pose a general ledger account should be opened entitled " Factory Space Account."

Now I am going to set out the principal working accounts in the general ledger of a machinery manufacturing business, in order that we may see just what they are and what their relations to each other are, and in order to bring out clearly the point at which we have arrived in considering their character and the manner of keeping them, and in order to see what accounts remain to be considered.

First, we have the three accounts which represent the stock of materials, and goods in process of manufacture, and finished goods. I have described the stores account fully to you, and I have partly described the manufacturing account, and I have, I think, pretty fully indicated the way in which the finished stock account is kept, the manner of keeping it being indeed parallel with the manner of keeping the stores account.

Then there are the accounts representing the cost of factory space, being as I have just said, the accounts for interest on investment in land and buildings, and for taxes on land and buildings, and for building repairs and depreciation and insurance, and for light and heat. And against these debit accounts we have the credit account entitled " Factory Space Account." ,

Then there are the accounts representing expenses of having and maintaining machinery, and the first of these expenses is the proportionate cost of factory-space, which may be charged to a " Machine Space Account." These accounts would therefore be:

Machine space.
Interest on investment in machinery.
Repairs to machinery.
Depreciation of machinery.
Taxes on machinery.
Insurance on machinery.
Special supplies.
Special superintendence.
Special tools expense.

And against these debit accounts we have the credit account entitled " Machine Rates Account."

And in the next place there are the accounts representing the cost of power. The first item in this cost is the charge for factory space occupied by the power plant, and a " Power Space

22

40

Account" may be opened to take this charge. These accounts will then be:

Power space.

Interest on investment in power plant.

Power plant repairs.

Power plant depreciation.

Fuels.

Water.

Firemen's wages.

Engineers' wages.

Power plant supplies.

And against these debit accounts we will open a " Power Credit Account," which will be credited with the cost of power as it is distributed. The way in which it is distributed is one of the things I want to describe to you this evening.

And then there is the storehouse expense account, of which I have spoken, and this is charged with the storehouse space, storehouse wages, and sundry storehouse expenses. It is also charged with interest on the average investment in materials in the storehouse.

I should perhaps have spoken before of the account to which interest on investment is credited when it is charged to the several divisions of the expenses. This account may be called " Interest Credit Account." It is credited with the interest on investment which is part of the factory space charge, and with that which enters into the machine rates, and with that which enters into the expense of power; and then with the interest charged to storehouse expense account; then with interest on the average goods in process of manufacture, which is part of the factory general expenses; and finally with interest on the capital employed at the selling end of the business, which is part of the commercial and not of the manufacturing expenses. So that this " Interest Credit Account " is credited with interest on all the capital employed in the business. Against this credit there will be found in the regular interest account the expense of interest on borrowed capital, and the difference between the two is interest on the capital stock which we started out to provide in our cost figures.

I think I ought to warn you that this is a method of my own, and that as far as I know it is not used except where I have used

23

it, and that it is without other authority, unless that authority be found in the logical necessities of the accounting, and in the practical usefulness of the method.

We now have certain remaining expenses which are purely general expenses, that is, general to the operations of the single department or individual shop, or general to the operations of the whole factory. The accounts for these may be:

Shop No. 1, general expense.

Shop No. 2, general expense.

Factory general expense.

And the charges to these, and the manner of absorbing these expenses in the cost accounts, is another thing I want to talk to you about this evening.

I have as yet said nothing about the labor accounts. The whole subject of directly productive labor I hope to take up in my next and final talk to you. The treatment of indirect or general labor will be practically covered by what I say this evening concerning the treatment of department, or individual shop, general expenses, and factory general expenses.

Of course directly productive labor is distributed to the cost accounts for the various products, exactly as the labor is recorded as being expended on each; and of course the total of it is charged to the manufacturing account in the general ledger, which must be kept in agreement with the cost accounts. When this is done, and the distribution of the power expense is complete, and the distribution of indirect, or general expenses, is complete, the cost accounts and the debit side of the manufacturing account will be pretty nearly complete also.

If a power plant consisted of one or more boilers supplying steam solely to one or more engines developing power to be transmitted by a common means for the purpose of running the machinery of a single manufacturing plant, and if, as I suggested in my last lecture, no distinction should be made in the cost of the unit of power, which we will consider as the horse-power hour, at the machines, whether the power were transmitted a greater or a lesser distance, we could very easily make a distribution of the power expense to the various cost accounts. Knowing the total of the power expense, it would be necessary to ascertain as closely as possible the units of power delivered at the machines, and dividing the expense by the number of units, charge the respective

24

operations with the resulting figure, multiplied by the number of horse-power taken by the machine in operation, multiplied by the running time of the machine.

There are two ways to ascertain more or less closely the units of power delivered at the machines. One is for the engineer to make a series of determinations of the power developed by the engine, and of the power lost in transmission, to arrive at the power delivered at the machines, these determinations being of sufficient number, and taken at such times, and over a sufficient period of time, so that the average of them shall pretty surely represent the average operation of the shops. And the other is to determine as closely as possible what power each machine takes, on an average of its operations, when actually running, and then to get a record of the running time over a sufficient period, and arrive at one's conclusion by this apparently more direct but still fallible method. By using the two methods in conjunction with each other, and each with care and perseverance, one could doubtless arrive at pretty correct figures.

But the distribution of the power expense is less simple than this, because as a rule the operations of a power plant are of a less simple character. Moreover, the method outlined would by no means be in conformity with the principle of analytical cost accounts, inasmuch as it merely aims to determine a cost figure, and not to show with all the clearness possible the conditions which are affecting the cost.

Steam is generally used from the boilers for more than a single purpose. It may be used for heating, or for the operation of pumps, or for the operation of two or more engines used for eutirely different purposes, or for all of these. It is absolutely necessary under these circumstances to get some measure of the steam furnished by the boilers for the several purposes for which steam is furnished.

For the two purposes of the accounts, viz.: to constantly control the efficiency and the economy of the operations, and to accurately determine and distribute costs, it is necessary first that a current record be made of the steam produced, and the conditions under which it is produced, and the cost of producing it; that is, of the coal consumed, and the water evaporated, and of the temperature of the water that goes into the boilers, and of the boiler pressures. Then a record must be kept of the engines

25

operated, and the power developed must be arrived at as closely as possible by the means I have described, and the pounds of steam used by each engine for each unit of horse-power developed must be determined, and so an account made of steam consumption to set against the record of steam produced.

It is, however, necessary to make an initial and tentative distribution of the steam expense on the basis of an engineer's calculations, just as the power charges are first made in the cost accounts on the basis of such calculations. If careful and thorough records are kept, the credits for steam and the credits for power set up on the basis of these calculations, will be compared with the records of steam and power generated and with the cost of the same, and calculations will be gradually corrected.

The steam expense of course includes the charge for boiler space and fuel storage space, and interest on the investment in boilers, and all the expenses of operating the boilers and keeping them in repair, and writing depreciation off from them. The total steam expense having been arrived at and divided up in the first place according to the engineer's calculations of the ways in which the steam is used, we have the beginning of our calculation of the cost of power furnished to the machines.

The cost of power furnished by an engine consists of the proportionate charge against the engine for factory space, interest on the investment in the engine, expense of operating, and repairs and depreciation, and the cost of steam used. The total of these being arrived at, and the average power developed by the engine and the average power consumed in transmission having been determined, the total expense is divided by the horse-power calculated to be available at the machines, and the cost per horse-power is arrived at.

You will remember that I said to you that while it is somewhat laborious to determine accurately the expense of the individual machine per annum in order to arrive at a just hourly machine-rate, nothing is simpler than the use, in the cost accounts, of the machine-rates, once determined. In the same way, while it is somewhat laborious to determine even approximately the cost of the unit of power taken by the machines, the use in the cost accounts of this figure, once determined, is as simple as making any other conceivable charge in the costs accounts to represent the expense of power. And while in all factory accounting it must

26

be carefully aimed to secure economy in the current work, pains must not be spared in the occasional and special work which should give the current work both simplicity and soundness.

We now have the engineer's calculation of the average power taken by each machine when running, and we have a calculation of the cost of the unit of power at the machines. We need a record of the actual running time of the machines, and we can then make the charge for power in the various cost accounts, charging the total to the general ledger manufacturing account and crediting it to the general ledger "Power Credit Account."

You will remember that I told you that the labor tickets made out by every workman doing directly productive work for each job worked on, show the workman's number, and the job, and the machine tool used, and the time; and that this information is transcribed on the workman's weekly sheet where his wages are determined, and that the postings of machine time are made from these weekly sheets to the machine rates ledger, in which an account is kept for each machine, and that from the machine rates ledger postings of machine rates are made to the cost accounts.

I want now to explain to you how the power charge is brought into the machine rates ledger, and how the posting from the machine rates ledger to the cost accounts includes both the machine rate and the power rate.

We have the total time the machine is engaged on the job, and inasmuch as the machine is not actually running the whole of this time, we need to know the non-running time in order to deduct it and arrive at the time for which power is chargeable.

For this purpose a record of the non-running time is kept in the shops. The sheet used for the purpose is like this:

NON-RUNNING TIME—WEEK ENDING...

Workman's Number	Job No.	Machine No.	From		To		Extension	
			Day	Hour	Day	Hour	Hrs.	Min.

And now I want to show you the complete machine rates ledger form:—See Figure 1 next page.

As far as the "Total Time" column the entry is made from the workmen's weekly wages sheets, and the "Power Time" is arrived at by taking the non-running time sheet for the same

27

45

MACHINE NO. ....

Machine Rate ....Power ....h.p. Rate ....

Workman	Job	From			To			Total Time		Power		Exten-sion	Posted Cost Ledger
		Day	Hr.	Min.	Day	Hr.	Min.	Hrs.	Min.	Hrs.	Min.		

week and deducting the non-running time recorded for the particular job and the particular machine.

It is not attempted to record on the non-running time sheet every little interruption of the running. The plan is to make a record of the time taken to adjust machines for the jobs, and to put the materials in the machines; and of the time elapsing after the machine stops running until it is actually released for the next job; and in no case to record non-running time under a certain limit, at which it is seen that the difference in the power charge begins to be immaterial.

You will see that the accuracy of all extensions and all footings in the machine rates ledger can be easily proved by extending the footings of total time and power time at the respective rates at the head of the account.

And further, concerning the machine rates ledger, I will repeat to you what I said last week, changing it only so as to include the power item which I was excluding then, because I had not yet explained it to you:

" The charges of machine time and of power having been posted to the machine rates ledger for a given period, which it is convenient to make even weeks instead of the month, inasmuch as the postings are made from weekly sheets, a statement is drawn off from this ledger in the following form:

Machine No.	Time Charged	Amount	Idle Time	Amount	Power

the idle time for each machine being, of course, the difference between the time charged, and, if the period is a four weeks' period, four fifty-second parts of the number of hours into which the machine expense for the year was divided. Then a journal entry is made:

28

——Dr.——   ——Cr.——

Manufacturing Account
Idle Capacity Account

Machine Rates Account
Power Credit Account

the debit to the manufacturing account being for the charged machine time and the power, these being what are posted into the cost accounts."

And now it is necessary that I describe to you the ruling of the cost accounts, because I am coming to the matter of the charges in these accounts for indirect expenses; and as the charges of indirect expenses are based on two or three classes of direct charges separately, it is necessary to provide separate columns for these different classes of direct charges, so that the total of each may be readily available and the charges for indirect expenses made accordingly.

The form of the cost ledger account will then be something like this:

SHOP ORDER NO.···

    FOR···

    ···

Date	Particulars	Materials	Direct Labor	Machine Rates	Sundries	Total Dr.	Total Cr.

Now the storehouse expense account, which, as I have told you, consists of the charge for factory space, storehouse wages and sundry expenses, and the charge for interest on the average investment in materials in the storehouse, is absorbed in the cost accounts by charging a percentage on the total of the materials column. This percentage corresponds to the ratio between the annual storehouse expense and the value of the materials drawn out of store in the course of the year.

Next we have the department, or individual shop, expense accounts. These consist in each case of the department foreman's wages, the wages of any clerks in the department, and any other wages of purely indirect and general labor; then the expense of sundry general supplies; then a proportion of the expense of the tool department furnishing small tools for general uses to the departments as they need them, and receiving them back from the departments when the purpose for which they were obtained is fulfilled. And finally any other purely general expenses of the department.

And then there is the factory general expense, which includes all manufacturing expenses which not only cannot be connected with any particular job, but that also cannot be connected with any particular department. Such are the general superintendent's salary, and the charge for factory space for the general factory offices, the wages of watchmen and timekeepers, and interest on the average investment in work in process.

Each department, of course, bears its own general expenses, and the productive departments together bear the factory general expenses. The basis of distribution which I shall propose is the same in the two cases.

You will see that we have clearly established the incidence of a very large part of the total factory expenses, and that there is nothing left but expenses which have no special traceable incidence, and that must be regarded as falling on all the operations impartially. The operations are operations of men and machines, the machine expense rising and the labor expense falling, or the machine expense falling and the labor expense rising throughout. So intimately are these two expenses related to and dependent upon each other that they were, in a quotation I read to you in my first lecture, called together the "total labor cost." I do not therefore propose to separate them, choosing one and rejecting the other, when I need figures which are representative of the total operations as a basis for the distribution of expenses which, as I have said, are without any special traceable incidence, and must be regarded as falling on all the operations impartially.

The charge for the general expenses of a department is therefore made by means of a percentage corresponding to the ratio between the total machine rates in the department plus the total direct labor to operate the machines fully, and the amount of the department general expenses; and this percentage is added in the cost accounts to the direct labor and machine rates of that department.

And the charge for the factory general expenses is made by means of a percentage corresponding to the ratio between the total machine rates in the factory plus the total direct labor to operate the machines in the factory fully, and the amount of the factory general expenses; and this percentage is added in the cost accounts to all the direct labor and machine rates.

In practice the two percentages are combined. That is to say, if the general expense percentage for Department No. 1 were 20 per cent. and for Department No. 2 25 per cent., with the general factory expense 20 per cent., then in the cost amounts the only figure used would be 40 per cent. to add to direct labor and machine rates in Department No. 1, and 45 per cent. to add to direct labor and machine rates in Department No. 2.

It will be noticed that these debits to the cost accounts are not posted from a statement previously compiled, but originate in the cost ledgers. It is therefore necessary to create a record of them, and this is done by having an account in the cost ledgers headed general expense credits, and when the debits are made in the cost accounts, corresponding credits are made in this general expense credits account in the cost ledger, and the total of them is thence journalized for the general ledger, as follows:

Manufacturing Account
To General Expense Credit Account.

so we have a general expense credit account in the general ledger also.

Now you will notice that the percentages for general expenses were determined on the basis of full operation of the machines, and consequently a full pay-roll. How much the month's machine rates charged and actual pay-roll fall short of the full figures used as a basis can be easily ascertained, and the percentages upon the differences in the respective departments figured and a journal entry made for the amount:

Idle Capacity Account
To General Expense Credit Account.

Then the idle capacity account is charged with the whole expense of idle capacity, and the machine rates ledger shows just what capacity idle is resulting in that expense; and the cost figures are freed from the fluctuating and confusing element of the expense of capacity idle that ought to be operated; and profits are determined on the basis of these cost figures; but against these profits is always set out the idle capacity expense that has to be deducted from them, giving thus the net result of the operations, subject always to certain adjustments of values that have to be made in respect of any shrinkages from the book value of any current assets.

31

Factory Accounting as Applied to Machine Shops.

V.

By John Whitmore.

It must be borne in mind that these articles are written without any pretense of any knowledge beyond that of the accountant. If matters that have generally been regarded as outside of the province of the accountant are here treated, it is upon the principle already insisted upon, that if any true organization is to be accomplished it must be through the departments working up to each other with an intelligent appreciation of the way in which the work of each must merge into the harmonious working of them all to a single end. The work of every department is the affair of every other department, so far as each department can develop an understanding of the work of the others and facilitate it, and help to give it an increased efficiency. It is, for instance, very essential that this should be the attitude of the engineering department to the accounting department. It is an illustration of the way in which this principle has not been grasped, that engineers, realizing how many and intricate considerations must enter into the true determination of costs, and seeing no adequate sign that bookkeepers and accounting departments are equipped to deal with the matter, have claimed that "cost finding is an engineering problem." The bookkeeper, on the other hand, knows that the complete expenses of even the shop operation are disclosed only in the financial books, and knows the necessity of balanced bookkeeping wherever omissions are to be guarded against. Again it is plain that unless by "cost-finding" is meant the estimating of costs, there is a great deal of unmistakable bookkeeping work to be done.

The elements of cost so far dealt with are the simpler ones. That is to say, upon examination the method of dealing with them is plain. At scarcely any point are the figures absolutely final, free from all qualification and all contingencies, but the latter are recognizable, and, generally speaking, arise from uncertainties that are a condition of the work done. This does not mean that the cost figures arrived at are necessarily of limited value from these causes. For instance, so long as the life of a machine cannot be accurately foreseen, the best judgment concerning it is the fact to be dealt with. On the other hand fictitious cost figures might be created through machine parts being produced in

106

quantities larger than the existing requirements justify, and so obtaining a nominally low cost for those actually used at the expense of having later to write down the value of those which become inactive stock. The means of guarding against such a condition and the means of safeguarding the accuracy of all one's figures, and so giving them the fullest value, have so far been indicated.

The problem is somewhat changed when one comes to the accounting for small tools, and patterns, and drawings. These it is now proposed to consider.

Advantageous working of the shops and accuracy in the cost accounts are alike dependent upon the sound organization of the tool department. The shop necessity of the prompt furnishing of needed tools is the same as the necessity of the prompt furnishing of needed materials. Clearness in the tool records is necessary to the prompt furnishing of small tools to the machines, and to the accuracy of the small tool charge in the respective cost accounts, and to the economical administration of the tool department itself.

Small tools may from the accounting standpoint be divided into three classes: 1. Those that are made for the purpose of a particular product, that is not a standard product or, in other words, that are made for a special job or contract and whose further use is problematical. The production order for such tools must show distinctly the job for which they are produced and the cost account to which they are directly chargeable. 2. Tools whose use is limited to a single machine or a limited group of machines and whose repair and depreciation charges can consequently be covered in the machine rates for such machines. 3. Tools whose use is of such a general character that their repair and depreciation charges are not traceable as expenses of certain machines, but may with fidelity to actual conditions be regarded as general expenses of one, or more than one, or all of the shop departments.

For the purpose of small tool records, doubtless the card index is the most useful and convenient device. Such an index, or, more properly, card ledger, should be kept for all the tools belonging to the tool room, including all its branches. This ledger may be divided into three divisions, or into three ledgers, corresponding to the three divisions of the small tool equipment set out above.

107

51

The accounts should show the location of the tools and their inventory value, and the ledgers should be kept in agreement with the controlling tool accounts in the general ledger.

The first class of small tools mentioned, being those whose cost is properly charged into the cost of the job for which they are made, but which, while their cost has been written off, are kept for possible future use, although that may be limited to repairs and renewals or extension of the original job, may have a nominal value placed upon them. If their future use is very uncertain it would be best in setting up such values to make the corresponding credit to a reserve account, so as not at all to reverse in the profit and loss account the first treatment of the expenditure as part of the job cost. Any reliable value that there is in such tools may, of course, be credited to the job cost to which the tools were charged.

The card ledger accounts for tools of the second class should be arranged in divisions corresponding to the several departments of the shops, and each account should show the machine tool or machine tools to which the small tools represented belong, and the heading of the account might include a summary of the actual uses of the tools. Such tools being presumably stored in the departments where they are used, duplicates of the several divisions of the ledger may advantageously be created and kept in the respective departments.

The records of the third class are confined to the tool department, the tools represented being kept in the general tool room, from which they are distributed as occasion for their use arises. When these tools are out of the tool room it is customary, and necessary to their control, to have them represented by two checks, the first identifying the tool and the second bearing the number of the workman in whose charge it is. The accounts in this ledger should be very carefully classified and arranged so as to constitute the clearest possible statement of the small tool equipment represented.

The next record in relation to small tools is a card index of the standard parts machined in each department respectively, stating all the tools required for the processes in each case, and stating their location. This facilitates the prompt delivery to a machinist of all the tools proper to be used upon a given job. There is then in each department of the shops a cross index, to

108

the tools kept in the department and their uses, and to the parts to be machined and the tools proper to the operations.

Additional tools are produced under numbered production orders for which cost accounts are kept in a plant production cost ledger. Tool repairs and replacements may be done under numbered repair orders if the operation is large enough, and it is well to fix a limit of estimated expense or for small repairs under standing tool repair orders. The series of standing tool repair orders must correspond to the distribution of the tool expense which it is found practicable to make in the cost accounts either through machine rates or department expense accounts. Closed cost accounts for tool production and tool repairs should, after all entries are made in the general books, be filed away in the tool department, and these accounts should be kept in such detail as would enable the management of the tool department to readily obtain from them any information that in experience might be found useful and obtainable by this means.

There would then have been created a full and completely classified record of the small tool equipment, with locations, uses, and values; and full and available records of tool production; and completely classified records of the expense of tool repairs and renewals; facilitating the shop operations and making possible accuracy in the accounting; and at the same time surely creating facilities for the management of the tool department to the ends of maintaining the necessary equipment without duplication, and watching and controlling the tool repair expense; and possibly for the more technical purposes of standardizing tools and regulating the materials used in their manufacture.

The organization and the accounting in relation to foundry patterns are simpler than the corresponding matters in relation to small tools, but there is none the less the necessity for absolutely clear records and strict methods of procedure. This is, of course, especially true where the shops are large and the product of a varied and varying character, and the active or semi-active patterns consequently large in number, and again where there is added to these conditions that of the castings being made by independent foundries. The expense direct and indirect of any mistake in furnishing patterns to the foundry is inevitably serious, and the methods used should carefully safeguard this matter.

The first necessity is a pattern ledger, and for this purpose a loose-leaf ledger is probably the most convenient device. It is

109

most desirable that the pattern numbers be continually maintained in a certain intelligible order; that is, that a series of consecutive numbers be assigned to each class of product of the shops, and then that the cast iron parts entering into each such class of product be classified, and each series of numbers divided up in accordance with this sub-classification. If this arrangement of numbers is to be kept undisturbed through a period of years, there must be blank numbers for future use in every subdivision. These are conditions under which the loose-leaf book is especially useful.

Castings accounts in the storehouse ledgers should be in the same order as the corresponding pattern accounts in the pattern ledgers. This arrangement of numbers greatly facilitates the work in the several departments, and if the original scheme is carefully worked out the numbers may be given so much significance that there is great likelihood of an inaccurate pattern number being recognized as inaccurate and the mistake corrected before it has caused any real trouble.

Each account in the pattern ledger should be headed with the pattern number and a general description of the pattern, and with the drawing number; and inasmuch as this is a permanent and always easily accessible record, it is well to add a complete list of the parts making up the pattern. Provision must be made for inserting the cost and for writing depreciation off from it. The balance of the page, or section of a page devoted to a single pattern, is to be used for recording its location and every change in location. This ledger will therefore tell all about a pattern, including where it is at any given time. If more than one foundry is casting for the shops it will furnish a record of the foundry or foundries which have made the castings.

Another matter of importance is that wherever a standard casting is to be varied, and there is consequently an alteration to be made in the pattern, the altered pattern shall bear a new number and a new account in the pattern ledger be opened for it, the old account being closed with a reference to the new number. When the pattern is altered back to the original form the temporary account is closed and the original account reopened.

Patterns that are made for the purposes of a special job or contract must, of course, be charged to the job cost account, as in the case of special tools, and thereafter treated upon the same principle as such tools and by a similar method. The cost of altering a pattern for a special job and the cost of altering it back to its standard form must be charged to the job cost account.

Separate pattern accounts should be kept in the general ledger representing the value of existing standard patterns for each distinct class of machinery or apparatus manufactured, and each of these pattern accounts would be kept in agreement with the corresponding section of the pattern ledger, both being charged with the original cost and having the same depreciation written off from them from time to time. Separate pattern repair accounts should be kept corresponding to the several capital pattern accounts.

If, then, a column is provided in the cost ledger form for rough castings, there can be added to the total of this column such a percentage as will provide for the repairs and depreciation of patterns for the class of product to which the cost account relates, plus the proportion of the general expenses of the pattern department chargeable to such class of product on the basis of the relation of the castings used in it to the total castings used in the total product. The conditions in relation to castings used in any shop need to be carefully considered in order to determine whether a further classification of patterns and the expenses attaching to their use needs to be made in order to insure the fairness of the pattern expense charge in all cost accounts.

If the patterns are sent to outside foundries it is necessary that they should be systematically checked up, with lists of all the parts of which they consist, both when they are shipped out and when they are received back. The ordinary precautions taken to insure the provision of all materials in readiness for the shop operations need to be taken with especial strictness in regard to castings made by outside foundries, as the conditions of their accurate and prompt production are obviously less simple.

The accounting in relation to the work of engineers and draftsman must be based upon the strictest possible record of the actual expenditure of their time. As far as their time is expended for the purposes of specific jobs it is, of course, charged to the job cost accounts. Beyond this it needs to be classified according to the various classes of product, and according to the particular purposes of the work. Some part of it will be a purely commercial expense, being for the purposes of prospective jobs. Some part of it will be for experimental and development work and will be a general charge against the profits of the business. Some part of it will be for the production of drawings for standard machines of each class of the product. This last it is proper to capitalize in accounts representing the value of the standard drawings for each class of the shop product. From these accounts depreciation must be regularly written off at annual rates sufficiently high to keep the drawing accounts from growing, in any case, out of proportion to the growth of the business, and, generally speaking, at rates somewhat higher than this, and these depreciation charges are general expenses of the manufacturing for the respective classes of the product. The general expenses of the engineering department are probably most justly included in the group of administration and office expenses, but emphasis may again be laid upon the necessity of strict time records, so that nothing may remain to be dealt with as general expenses that can be properly charged as a part of the cost of a specific job, or of a particular class or department of work.

It is not to be presumed that the operations of any shops will proceed along strictly routine lines. All operations have their peculiar features and are subject to various exigencies. It may be safely asserted that it is never necessary and that it is always dangerous to conduct any manufacturing operations in such a manner that the essential record cannot be made, for such operations would be simply disorderly. And with patience simple accounting methods can be developed to meet whatever special conditions exist. It is proposed to take as an illustration the necessity, which probably arises at times in all shops, of borrowing either from work in process or from finished stock some materials or some part of a machine which is so urgently needed as to justify extraordinary means of delivering it quickly. Here is something to be done which is not instructed by any shop order. The logical procedure is to issue a shop order which is, and is called, a borrowing order. Like every other series of shop orders, these are consecutively numbered and a cost account is opened for each. At the same time that the borrowing order is issued there is issued a production order to replace the part borrowed. This production order instructs that the expenditure under it be charged to the borrowing order. If the borrowing is from an

112

assembled machine the charges to the cost account consist of: 1. The labor, and other expense, if any, of detaching the part and getting it ready for its new use. 2. The cost of replacing the part and putting it back. If the borrowing is from unassembled parts, the borrowing order authorizes and makes a record of the borrowing, but the charges to the borrowing order cost account are only those incurred under the order to reproduce. In either case the cost account shows the actual cost of furnishing the part by means of borrowing it and replacing it.

And when all storehouse records and records of shop operations have been provided, together with the means of summarizing them for entry in the general books, there remains to be considered the important matter of the arrangement of the accounts in the general ledger. Whether beyond the monthly trial balance there is prepared each month a *pro forma* profit and loss account and balance sheet or not, it is still desirable that the ledger balances, as they follow each other in ledger and trial balance, shall be as plain and easily read a statement of the progress and condition of the business as it is possible to make them. Monthly profit and loss accounts and balance sheets are most desirable and are perfectly practicable so far as completed work goes. In the larger machine shops and engineering works there will always be a considerable number of open shop orders under which partly manufactured materials are being produced for the storehouse, and there will be job orders for equipment or installations which extend, from the beginning to the completion of them, over many months. In the latter case profits are in abeyance, and profit and loss account and balance sheet are subject to this fact. Again. there is the question of the feasibility of adjusting all open cost accounts each month in respect of all the general expenses of manufacturing. Wherever the conditions permit, and in many, and possibly in most, manufacturing businesses they do permit, the practical closing of the accounts at the end of each month there is no doubt of the value of doing it. Where many matters must, except at greater than monthly intervals, remain open, it does not mean that the situation is not to be very carefully gauged each month, but rather that it needs to be done with special care and perhaps special skill.

The arrangement of the accounts in a ledger should include the grouping of such accounts as are anywhere dealt with or to be considered in their total, and the placing in proximity to each other of figures whose relationship to each other it is necessary to watch. All the accounts representing the cost of factory and yard space should be brought into a group, and there should immediately follow this group the account credited with the distribution of these expenses. If an inside column be provided in the trial balance where such groups of expenses can be footed it will immediately be seen whether such expenses are running more or less than the calculation concerning them. Similarly with all the expenses which it is planned to absorb into the cost accounts by means of machine rates, and with the account to which the machine rates are credited; and again with all the expenses that make up the cost of power, and with the power credit account. So far, there is a complete distribution or absorption of expenses monthly. Coming to the department and factory general expenses, the administration and office expenses, and the trading expenses, if the work of the shops is of a fairly even character and does not include jobs that are in process for lengthy and irregular periods, there will easily be established an approximate relationship between expenses incurred in each group and the same as absorbed in the cost accounts, the unabsorbed balance being in respect of work in process, and its reasonableness subject to not difficult proof. In cases where the work of the shops is not of an even character and some of the work is a long time in process, a calculation can be made in regard to the unabsorbed balances of general expenses by making the analyses necessary to determine to what parts of the bases of their distribution such general expenses have been applied and consequently what parts of them await the addition of the general expense percentages in the cost accounts. It is, for instance, not a very difficult matter to ascertain the amount of the direct labor pay-roll and the machine rates in a given department, and the credits to general manufacturing expenses in respect of that department's labor and machine rates, and from the percentage in use to calculate the further credit which would come from that department in an adjustment of the cost accounts to date. Where the use of thorough accounting methods has prepared the way, the analysis and summing up of the showing of the monthly trial balance is an excellent test of the efficiency of the head of the accounting department.

Factory Accounting as Applied to Machine Shops. VI.*

By John Whitmore.

It may be taken for granted that one of the chief ends to be striven for in the organization of a factory is the perfect co-ordination of the work of the several departments so that friction, in its simplest sense, may be eliminated. It has perhaps been made plain that in order to achieve this not merely mutual good-will is necessary, but a strong effort at mutual understanding, and the careful working out of inter-departmental routine. These three requisites are perhaps most often created in exactly the reverse of the order stated. If the relations between the departments are properly established, mutual understanding and help-fulness, and the sense of a common effort should inevitably follow.

The principle that cordial co-operation is a great gain is doubtless universally recognized. Its application so far would probably be undisputed. The question to be broached and a little considered here is whether it is not of equally unrestricted application when the co-operation is that between employer and employed, or whether it ceases to be applicable because interests are no longer the same, but are conflicting.

There is no doubt that the interests of employer and employed are identical to this extent; that waste, if it goes far enough, will be fatal to both, and that it is impossible to be sure that any waste injures only the one, or only the other. The conflict must be assumed to come in the division of the return secured by employer and employed, by the capital of the former, and the labor of both, in combination, and not to be as to the common desirability that the return available for division shall be as large as possible. But, under modern factory conditions, can the two matters ever be separate? Will the total return to employer and employed ever be the same with one scale and system of wages as with another?

There is nothing new in the proposition that larger profits to capital may be secured by paying higher wages. The contention is at the basis of every premium or bonus or profit sharing system. It is possible perhaps to take the narrow view that such plans are a coaxing of a somewhat refractory element to do its best. The

*This is the last installment of Mr. Whitmore's series of articles.

211

broader view is that first the stirring of ambition and hope, and ultimately changed physical conditions, make possible good work which otherwise was not possible.

Again, no employer believes that it is desirable for wages to fall below a certain point, at the lowest the point at which it is possible for the laborer to maintain a certain physical efficiency. If the work to be done is purely physical, and if there is no better and no worse to it, and if its quantity can be insured, there is an apparent gain in paying no higher wages than will suffice to the end stated. Moral considerations have, however, some standing, else one might urge the supreme economy of stealing one's raw materials if one could only find out a way to do it safely. There is indeed a close parallel between the underpayment of labor and stealing, inasmuch as in each there is or may be a material gain made for one's self at the cost of a measure of destruction probably both material and moral to others.

There is a very general, perhaps a universal, recognition on the part of employers that the fullness of value received for wages paid increases as the wages rise. It troubles no employer if he lose men to whom the lowest wages are paid. Concerning men to whom high wages are paid there is a feeling that they are valuable, that one cannot afford to lose them. Where the highest salaries are paid there is not infrequently so keen a sense of the profit to the employer that he insures the life of the employee. It may be said that one is indifferent about losing the cheaper labor because it can be most readily replaced, but that is only another aspect of the fact that it is the least profitable labor to buy.

The wages that can be paid to any man are obviously limited by two conditions: first, the opportunity for valuable work in the position held, and second, the ability of the man to avail himself of the opportunity. And nothing in the whole matter seems clearer than that the higher the wages that are justified and paid, the greater the profit to both employer and employed.

Modern factory conditions, including the high value of the machinery employed, and the constant improvements in processes resulting in constantly new situations, in each of which new opportunities for further improvements still are discovered, and the mutual dependence of all departments and all workmen because of the specialization of labor, these seem to open up to almost or quite everyone engaged in manufacturing operations an incomparably greater range than formerly of responsibilities and possibilities of usefulness. These possibilities of usefulness depend, however, for anything like a full development of them upon an able and wise organization. The work of organization includes the taking stock of the resources at one's command and planning the fullest use of them all. One of these resources is likely to be cash and another the intelligence of employees, and the organization is imperfect which allows either of these to be unused or only partially used when the need for their full use exists.

The existence of unused resources in the intelligence of subordinate employees in factories has been of later years recognized to a considerable extent, and hence the not uncommon standing offers of prizes to workmen for suggestions which prove of value. The idea is undoubtedly a sound one; the method of giving it effect impresses one as elementary. The appeal is certainly a simple one; the response, according to all accounts, is always, or almost always, worth while.

Without questioning the stimulus given by the opportunity to earn more money, it may be confidently said that it is not of itself adequate to the securing of the desired end. It may be even doubted whether this appeal constitutes the right starting point in the matter. The fullest response is likely to come where more is first asked of men, not in volume of physical labor, but in thoughtfulness and judgment and the sharing of responsibilities. Out of the attitude so created the maximum physical effort comes naturally. And upon the full exercise of all a workman's abilities there must follow an adequate rise in his wages, and as an element in this, and perhaps a very important one, there may be included a constant adjustment of the wages paid upon the basis of certain results produced.

If a superintendent of a shop were to single out one workman of average ability, and develop a practice of talking over the shop problems with him, giving and asking opinions, such a workman probably ninety-nine times out of one hundred would respond warmly, and would presently be observing and considering more carefully, and forming new judgments and freely communicating them. It is worth while to consider whether such an effect could be created, not in relation to a single workman, but in relation to the whole of a force of workmen. Such a result must always depend to a great degree upon the largeness and saneness of mind possessed by superintendents and foremen, but this is a spirit that may be either developed or discouraged, and one favorable condition will have been created if the principle of appealing to the thoughtfulness and judgment of the individual workman can in some way be incorporated in the shop routine.

Inasmuch, however, as no feature of the shop organization which involves the relations between management and workmen, or employer and employed, can remain unaffected by the wage system, it will be well to consider this before arriving at any conclusions.

The commonest wage system in machine shops is doubtless the piece-work system. That paying according to the quantity of work done results in all or almost all workmen doing more than they do under a system of straight day wages is abundantly plain. Its adoption, too, has doubtless been favored by the fact that there is nothing complex in the idea or in the clerical work necessitated. The operation of the piece-work system in most shops is indeed too simple and does not include the painstaking necessary to either the fullest justice or effectiveness. There is often a failure to appreciate the time required to set the rates intelligently, and consequently the staff assigned to this work is inadequate. If rates are hastily set they may be too low and the workman has just grounds for protesting, and is then perhaps in many instances allowed his time rate, or they may be too high, and reductions follow. The commonest condition is that workmen come to recognize that if their earnings under any piece price are high the piece price will be lower thereafter, and output is likely to be regulated so as not to bring about reductions in the prices. The simplest remedy for these great defects would seem to be to set the piece prices after sufficiently careful calculation of the time occupied, and then to make them unchangeable for a considerable period, unless, of course, a process should be changed, and finally when the time comes for revision to make only absolutely necessary changes and with such liberality as would insure the assent of reasonable men.

An obvious shortcoming in the ordinary piece-rate system is that it make no distinction as to the time required on a job. That is, the labor value is taken to be the same whether the machine cost is increased or decreased by the workman being quicker or slower. This shortcoming, with others in ordinary piece-rate systems, was dealt with and probably overcome in what is known as the differential piece-rate system invented a number of years ago by Mr. F. W. Taylor, of Bethlehem, Pa. Under this system the piece prices are set with great care, being upon careful observations of the time required for each element of the job, and then the price is varied according to the time taken, the highest price being paid for the quickest work, or, in other words, the labor value being taken as highest when the machine cost is kept at its lowest. Of course, whenever time consumed on the respective jobs is affecting the day's wages, efficient inspection is especially necessary, prices being set for good work and not for bad work.

The second widely used plan of paying machine shop labor is the premium plan. This plan also was invented many years ago and has doubtless been infinitely varied in actual use. The original idea was to fix a reasonable average time for each job and to pay the workman his hourly rate for the time spent on the job, and if the time consumed was less than the time set to give the workman part of his wages for the time not consumed. If time is set no higher than would be taken without the premium feature of the wages the gain to the employer is twofold; first, a lower labor cost, and second, a lower machine cost. The gain to the workman is everything paid to him as premium, inasmuch as his hourly rate is undisturbed.

The fact that under the premium plan the hourly rate is undisturbed is the essential difference between the piece-work plan and the premium plan, and I believe the difference is decidedly in favor of the premium plan. The responsibility is fairly placed upon the employer of paying a man the wage rate that properly belongs to his work or of dismissing him as unsatisfactory. The employer must assume this responsibility or suffer loss. If a poor workman earns low piece-rate wages and the matter is assumed to be all right because the wages correspond to the work done, the cost of the work is likely to remain very high because of the undue amount of machine expense.

In considering the value of labor in the various processes it is plain that the hourly machine costs are among the fundamental data. These costs are like money handled by the workmen carefully or carelessly, and foremost among the responsibilities of machine shop workmen is the efficient stewardship of these values. It is probable that very many and possibly the great majority of machinists would feel a quickening of interest and of the managing faculty if they merely knew the hourly expense, operated and idle, of the machines they are running. If this knowledge gave them an added sense of the value of their work in economizing machine time so much the better, and so wherever pertinent knowledge can be put in the place of ignorance.

Of course, the pre-requisite in the matter of establishing a standard of economy in regard to machine time, is such shop and commercial organization as shall insure that the job and the materials and the tools shall be promptly furnished to the machine operator when he is ready for them. To this end is the storehouse organization, and the tool-room organization, and the shop management.

The shop management which provides for the continuous operation of each machine is of the utmost importance. It would probably be, not an extravagance, but an economy to employ the necessary clerical labor in order to keep an account for each machine, entering the calculated time of every job ahead and offsetting the same time as each job is completed, so that the record would continuously show how many hours' work was provided in advance for each machine. The times fixed for the purpose of the premium payments would be available for such a record, and the work ahead for each machine could be regarded as subject to a deduction equal to the average gain of time upon which premiums are being paid. If the piece-work system were being used the time records in connection with the piece-work could be made available.

The following quotation from an article by Mr. John Ashford, entitled "The Tool Room and its Functions," which appeared in the *Engineering Magazine* of August, 1904, has an important bearing upon the matters now being dealt with: "That a given piece of work may be machined in the best and cheapest way, thought must be given to it and a series of operations fixed upon that seem the best, having due regard to the machines and tools available. This matter is often left to the foreman of a shop who, with his multifarious duties, cannot be expected to give adequate attention to it; neither can he mentally retain the particulars of processes and tools for a multitude of jobs, nor—for want of time even if he had the memory—can he impart them in detail to the men. It is therefore advisable for the operations to be placed be-

216

forehand by the tool draughtsman in conjunction with the works manager, and when fixed upon these operations, together with references to the tools, should be recorded in some permanent manner. . . . The operations when fixed upon can be noted, when possible, upon the drawing of the work to be made, but where too lengthy it can be typewritten and mounted upon cards."

The principle of appealing to the thoughtfulness and judgment of the individual workmen would be incorporated in the shop routine if space were provided on every such list of operations for suggestions of the machinist doing them as to any changes that he believes would be advantageous. The permanence given to the piece rates or time allowances, in accordance with which, unless a process were radically changed, rate or time would remain undisturbed throughout a certain period, would insure to a workman making a time saving suggestion the benefit in his wages. If such a suggestion resulted in a new piece rate or time allowance being set, another method of compensation might be arranged. Even if in some cases the direct benefit might go to the employer only, it could never do so at any expense to the employee, for that could not in justice be permitted. On the other hand, the direct benefit would almost always be common to both, and the sense of common interest and of the working together of managers and subordinates, and personal pride which is so often stronger than the desire of gain, would all tend to develop in the workmen the utmost anxiousness to justify the hope and belief manifestly placed in them.

It is not the intention here, it has not been the intention anywhere in these articles, to lay down cut and dried plans, but only to suggest and illustrate principles. If the principle of making available the knowledge and the judgment of every employee for the purpose of bettering processes and organization were established, the ways of making it effective would gradually unfold themselves. In its full development it might almost accomplish the elimination of waste in factory operations which otherwise seems hopeless. For there is no waste but falls under some one's eye, and no difficulty but some one knows of it, and probably there is no man but sees something which others fail to see. It needs only wise organization to open this great field for advantageous working together to all who are engaged in productive operations. Wise organization would include provision for measuring values with all possible accuracy, and especially labor values, and for paying increasing wages as services increased in value. Under such conditions high wages would be the surest means of obtaining a minimum cost of production.

There is in all productive operations a law of increasing and decreasing return whose workings are only followed by means of constant and patient analysis. When such analysis is applied to the complexities of modern manufacture, innumerable losses are found constantly eating into profits otherwise made. When the problem of eliminating such losses is considered it is plainly seen that the essential need is the organizing of every resource of brain and active interest, and the constant building up and co-ordinating of every human efficiency. In such a process wages would inevitably rise, for high wages are both a cause and an effect of high efficiency as low wages are both a cause and an effect of low efficiency. In such a process also the supposed antagonism between labor and capital might give way to a sense of common interest and common achievement.

The Proper Treatment of Machine Costs—A Criticism and a Theory

The Proper Treatment of Machine Costs.— A Criticism and a Theory.

By Andrew A. Murdoch.

I have read Mr. Whitmore's articles on Machine Shop Costs with much interest, and should like to be allowed to make a few comments, and at the same time to advance a new theory.

At the outset, let me state what I consider the simple analysis of a cost system.

There are three elements of direct or specific cost, the amounts of which must first be determined, as follows:

A. Material.

B. Manual labor.

C. Machine labor.

These being ascertained, all other charges and expenses can be identified as functions of one or more of them and assessed as a "loading" accordingly, until the total expenditure from start to finish has been properly and entirely distributed. This is really all there is to it, and it does not strike one as being surprisingly difficult or complex. In fact, neither the first nor the second of these elementary costs presents any difficulty, as the exact amount of money spent is a matter of book record in each case.

While this is so, I should like to state from my experience that there are very few firms in New York to-day who make any attempt to install a system of costs that is worthy of the name in respect of the method of charging out material. The material actually used on a job forms the basic element of the cost, the very foundation of the work without which the other two elements do not come into existence, and yet we find reputable firms of accountants installing cost systems based on a fixed "bill of material" which probably never agrees with the actual facts as regards value, which cannot possibly reflect the conditions under which goods are issued and returned, and which certainly does not in any way control or minimize the waste. Mr. Whitmore is strong on this point, and rightly so. It is no sort of cost system at all that does not deal with facts where facts are obtainable and that allows excess materials drawn from the storeroom to run riot over the various departments without being duly accounted for; and a client who allows accountants to delude him with the specious promise that their simple little "bill of material" method will save accountant's fees must be blissfully ignorant of the fact that on a proper system the saving from waste material alone would more than counterbalance the excess fees in less than a year, and continue as an increasing saving year after year.

Leaving material and manual labor as having been exhaustively treated, let us turn to the third element of direct cost. This element, called machine labor—though in a machine shop by far the most important—is not so easily determinable, for the reason that the work done by machines and tools is not directly measured or recorded. It is just around this problem of arriving at a reliable estimate of the value of such work that the first real difficulty crops out and leads into such labyrinthine elaboration. That the machine cost formulated by Mr. Whitmore is too involved to be practicable will be unhesitatingly admitted by every seeker after simplicity in accounting, and that on a closer examination it is in parts not sustainable on sound principle I shall try to prove in what follows:

The cost of manual labor may be said to be the rent for which workmen's services are obtainable, and the corresponding cost of machine labor is the rent for which we might be supposed to hire the machines. Such rent would be figured to cover:

1. Interest on value of machine.
2. Insurance and taxes.
3. Depreciation sinking fund.

In addition to these factors, which constitute the bare return to the owner on his investment, we should have to include the running expenses, as follows:

4. Power expense.
5. Operating and maintenance expense.

Mr. Whitmore insists on half a dozen other charges, in the name of "floor space," covering interest, insurance and taxes on value of land and building as well as repairs, depreciation and other expenses of maintaining the buildings; but these, in my humble opinion, are no more a part of the direct machine cost in a machine shop than they are of the direct labor cost in a factory where all the work is done by hand. Besides, even in a machine shop such charges should not be treated as being exclusively in respect of machines. The site and buildings have presumably been acquired as much for the purpose of sheltering and accommodating the employees and storing materials, as for affording " floor space " for the machines. They must therefore be considered as indirect or overhead costs, and, as such, assessed over all three elements of direct cost as a " loading " along with other charges of a similar nature in the manner described later in this article.

The next complication that spoils the simplicity of Mr. Whitmore's scheme is " crane service," the cost of which he thinks must be distributed over the machines served. Why? When a laborer handles materials between machines or departments there is no such complication. We either charge his time direct to the job or assess it as a general labor charge over the direct manual labor. So it is with " crane service." A crane is a machine, and its time should be reported as such and either charged along with other machine time direct to the jobs or assessed as a general labor charge over the direct machine labor.

Similarly we dispose of his item No. 8, " Proportion of Superintendence which is special to a limited number of machines." We much prefer to treat all manual labor as a separate and distinct element of direct cost as explained above. Even the wages of a foreman should be distributed to the work whenever it becomes apparent that he is spending more time on any particular job than is allowable as general superintendence.

Mr. Whitmore's final stumbling block is " expense of interest, repairs and depreciation on tools whose use is confined to the machine." As the original value of the machines includes a complete outfit of such tools; interest, repairs, and depreciation have therefore already been figured. If special tools are bought for a particular job, their cost must, of course, be entirely taken up by that job, unless there is a reasonable probability of their being used again, when a proportionate balance might be carried over in a separate cost ledger account to be absorbed later. But the whole question of loose tools is one which we feel perfectly safe in relegating to the " loading " class of costs to be imposed in a general percentage as a function of machine or manual labor, according as the tools operated are machine tools or hand tools. If we must enter into the cost of every one of some thousands of loose tools used in a large machine shop for the purpose of differentiating between fractional parts of a cent in the total

125

71

cost, we need not be surprised if our clients find reason to complain of the expense of the work of installing a system based on such futile elaboration. The whole cost of upkeep of loose tools in a machine shop does not exceed 5 per cent. of the total cost, and to attempt to identify and charge out the details of such a mass of minutiæ would result in additional costs appearing in the "loading" in respect of accountancy charges probably far in excess of the cost of all the tools in the shop.

Having now arrived at the conclusion that no further complication need be added to the above five items of machine cost, I shall briefly comment on each one with special reference to Mr. Whitmore's views.

1. Interest on Value of Machines. This is simply the annual income that would accrue from the ascertained value at the usual rate of interest. In his lecture printed in the November number of THE JOURNAL OF ACCOUNTANCY, page 23, Mr. Whitmore says: "I think I ought to warn you that this is a method of my own, and that as far as I know it is not used except where I have used it." As a matter of fact, I introduced the idea three years ago in connection with certain factory accounts.

2. Insurance and Taxes. This covers the annual premium in respect of fire insurance and the taxes payable by the owner.

3. Depreciation. According to Mr. Whitmore, this charge must be made to decrease yearly with the diminishing value of the machine. I prefer to assume, however, that the efficiency of a machine remains constant during the entire period of its operating life; that, in fact, its operating life is really the duration of its efficiency, and that consequently the charges for interest, insurance, taxes, and depreciation remain the same as long as the machine is capable of turning out work. This is strictly in line with the hypothesis that we are simply paying rent for the use of the machines during their working life, and is further supported by the argument that the value of the work done by a machine in any two hours, even years apart, will not vary to any appreciable extent. So long as a machine is kept in good working order it will turn out practically the same value of work per hour. When it ceases to perform efficient work it is time to dispose of it and buy a new machine, and the charge should be figured on this basis. Accordingly we should fix the future efficient life of each machine and determine therefrom a percentage of the value to adopt as an annual charge for replacement.

4. Power Expense. The ascertained annual expense of power, including maintenance and depreciation of plant, will form the charge for distribution over the full capacity horse-power hours of all the machines.

5. Operating and Maintenance Expense. This is purely a charge against costs in respect of actual operation, representing the tear and wear of running, which eventually necessitates expenditure on repairs or renewals. The actual cost of repairing such tear and wear cannot, however, be immediately ascertained for each job handled, as repair work done at any particular time may be in respect of the operations of the machine for weeks previous; so we are forced to establish a fixed charge from the ascertained annual expenditure required to maintain each machine in a proper state of efficiency, including oil and waste and other running expenses.

Having established the annual charges for each machine, as above, we proceed to figure equivalent hourly rates in the following manner:

Items 1, 2, and 3 are by nature " time " charges; that is, they accrue whether the machines are operating or not. We accordingly divide the total of the three by the number of working hours in the year, say 2,700, the result being the rate per hour to be charged to the cost accounts or to idle machine expense, according as the machine is operating or idle, and credited in total to interest, insurance, taxes, and depreciation reserve accounts in their respective proportions. Item 4, as already stated, is divisible over the full capacity horse-power hours, and the result, being multiplied by the individual machine horse power, will give the required hourly rate in respect of power to be charged to costs or idle machines expense and credited to power expense reserve account. Item 5, being purely an operating charge not incurred during idle time, is therefore only assessable over operating hours. We accordingly divide the ascertained year's expenditure by the actual number of hours which the machine ran, getting as a result the hourly rate to be charged to costs in respect of repairs and credited to maintenance reserve account.

The distinction proposed by Mr. Whitmore as between machines in general use and those used for special purposes only would virtually mean establishing an individual standard of full

127

capacity for every machine in the shop. In my opinion, such elaboration would not only be a hair-splitting proceeding, but would undoubtedly destroy much of the usefulness of the record of idle machines for purposes of comparison. A machine shop that installs special machines without being in a position to use their full capacity wants particularly to have the idle time shown up on the same basis as other machines, so as to get a line on the loss resulting from their installation.

The three elementary direct costs being now ascertained and established on a working basis, the second step is to segregate all factory expenses according as they are functions of one or other or more of these direct costs, in order to determine the percentages by which they may be most equitably absorbed.

The following is a rough schedule of such expenses arranged according to the direct costs on which they are naturally assessable:

A. *Material.*
  Interest on average investment.
  Purchasing department and storeroom expense.
  Note.—These expenses (which include rent, taxes, insurance, repairs, and depreciation in respect of storeroom, etc.) should be taken up in the value of the material when stocked.

B. *Manual Labor.*
  Employer's liability insurance.
  Hand tools expense.

C. *Machine Labor.*
  Machine tools expense.

* B *and* C.
  Foremen, timekeepers, and factory clerks' wages.
  Land and building expense (after charging off proportions for storeroom and offices) including rent, taxes, insurance, repairs and depreciation.
  Departments' general labor and expense.

* A + B + C + *foregoing percentages.*
  Superintendents' department salaries.
  Factory office expense.
  Factory general expense.

We are now in possession of what is known as "factory cost," and in order to evolve therefrom the total cost of production, it only remains as a third and final step to superimpose another loading to take care of expenses of administration. As these expenses often run to as much as 50 per cent. of the cost,

* Expenses marked thus are reduced to a full capacity basis; that is, the percentage is figured over the full output, and the balance not absorbed by the actual production is charged to "Idle Capacity Expense."

128

and cover the cost of governing both the production and selling departments, great care must be taken to obtain a correct classification of them. In the books all such expenses should be distributed over three columns, as follows: (1) production, (2) selling, (3) general.

The third column is used only when the expense cannot possibly be identified with either of the other two headings. Then, with a completed year's figures before us, we can prorate the third over the other two, and so arrive at a fairly safe estimate of the total overhead expenses chargeable against the year's production as well as those forming a deduction from the sales. The former is the figure which enables us to determine the full capacity percentage, which it will be necessary to add to the factory cost in order to arrive at the total cost, and further than this it is not necessary for us to go. We have now arrived at a satisfactory estimate of what we may call the legitimate or full capacity cost of our finished product. We tag it accordingly, and hand it over to the sales department, on whom devolves the duty of so adjusting the selling price that sufficient margin may be left between that and the cost to provide for selling expense and profit.

The only expense not taken care of is that arising from " Idle Capacity." The loading for profit must be made ample enough to cover this, as the selling department cannot be saddled with such expense specifically. The expense caused by machinery standing idle is the result of accident or bad management, and the proper cost figure to quote to the sales department for competitive purposes is the minimum at which the factory can produce the goods while running full swing, leaving it up to the executive to see that the production department keeps it down as near that minimum as possible.

It may be of interest to show that the above rather formidable looking array of percentages may always be reduced to three, one on each element of direct cost.

Using the letters A, B, C for the direct costs, as above, p^1, p^2, p^3, etc. for straight percentages, and f^1, f^2, f^3, etc., for full capacity percentages, we get the following formula for the factory cost:

$$F\ C = A+B+C$$
$$+p^1B+p^2C+f^1B+f^2C$$
$$+f^3(A+B+C+p^1B+p^2C+f^1B+f^2C)$$
$$=(1+f^3)A+(1+p^1+f^1+f^3+p^1f^3+f^1f^3)B+(1+p^2+f^2+f^3+p^2f^3+f^2f^3)C$$

Of course it follows that

Total Cost $= F\ C\ (1+f^4)$

which changes the co-efficients of A, B and C in proportion.

129

In this way we are able to establish a practicable plan for imposing the loadings, while it is an easy matter to resolve the resulting credits into their original factors when the time arrives for setting up the individual reserve accounts.

In conclusion, let me emphasize the increasing importance of recognizing machine labor as a basic element of cost. The tendency of the age is undoubtedly to supersede manual labor in every possible way by introducing machinery to do the work; so that while the direct pay roll becomes gradually less and less in proportion to the factory output, the expenditure on machinery keeps on growing more and more. The custom is to entirely ignore machine work as an element of direct cost, arbitrarily fixing the latter as composed only of material and manual labor and loading all machinery and power expense, including repairs and depreciation, as a percentage on the amount of manual labor only. As an evident consequence of this method, the more hand work we put on a job the more will be the loading for machinery expense, and the more actual machine work we introduce, the less will it bear of the loading; or to carry the anomaly to its legitimate limit, a job done entirely by hand would bear a full share of the machinery cost, whereas a job done exclusively on the machines would bear none.

As a concrete example, take the case of an automatic screw machine turning out small completed parts by the score every hour. Six such machines will barely occupy the time of one man, and on an ordinary cost system the product would be charged with a sixth part of his wages and loaded in proportion, whereas if the operations were entirely done by hand not only would the direct cost be more, but the loading for machinery expense would be proportionately greater, although, as a matter of fact, no machine work had been done at all.

Surely nothing more need be said to prove that the old method is incorrect and liable to produce misleading results, and to establish the principle that the work done by a machine must be measured and figured as one of the basic elements of prime cost, on the accuracy of which the whole superstructure depends.

Some Details of Machine Shop Cost Accounts

Some Details of Machine Shop Cost Accounts

By John Whitmore.

It may be well for me to reply, as briefly as possible, to Mr. Murdoch's criticism of the articles written by me which have recently appeared in The Journal. Mr. Murdoch takes up practically the single matter of the machine rate as I have described it and makes one general criticism of it, namely, that it is "too involved to be practicable," and a second, of which he later gives specifications, that it is "in parts not sustainable on sound principle." I will take up these specifications one by one.

Mr. Murdoch's first objection is to the floor-space item as part of the machine rate. He says "the site and buildings have presumably been acquired as much for the purpose of sheltering and accommodating the employees and storing materials as for affording floor-space for the machines." Mr. Murdoch will find that I have distributed the floor-space expense to storage, factory offices, general offices, non-machine space in shops, and machine space. His objection is presumably narrowed down to my treatment of the machine space. I have included it in the machine rates on the basis of the space occupied by the respective machines. This seems to me so obvious and simple a thing that it is almost inevitable if one attempts to distribute the charge in accordance with actual conditions. Whether Mr. Murdoch counts up men or machines, or both, or adds up machine hours or rates, or machinists' hours or wages, I doubt that he will evolve a basis for this distribution which because of superior simplicity or accuracy will supersede the one I adopted, and did not originate, and was glad to adopt.

The second objection is to the inclusion of crane service in the machine rate. Mr. Murdoch claims a parallel between this expense and the expense of laborers handling materials. Cranes are used for handling the heavier materials. They have to be operated by men; they do not dispense with men's labor. They appear to be manifestly a special and additional expense of handling heavy materials, and I believe actual observation of the work will leave no doubt of the fact. Mr. Murdoch says "a crane is a machine, and its time should be reported as such,

294

and either charged along with other machine time direct to the job, or assessed as a general labor charge over the direct labor." Here are two radically different methods: one to treat it as a direct job cost, the other as general indirect expense. I believe the first, by the method suggested, is quite impracticable, that is if the actual expense of the crane is to be absorbed and equitably divided between jobs; and I believe this result is accomplished in the same full sense by the method I suggested, which calls for no separate record of crane operations and so is far simpler. And I believe the alternative treatment suggested by Mr. Murdoch is wrong, unless there were in some rare cases such equal conditions throughout a shop that scarcely any averaging of expenses could be erroneous.

Mr. Murdoch goes on, " similarly we dispose of his item No. 8." This is superintendence which is special to a limited number of machines. Mr. Murdoch wants a direct distribution. All superintendents, however, insist that they cannot record their time as between separate jobs, and I think they are clearly right. Moreover, for reasons it would take some time to go into fully, such a record would be of little, if any use. The method I adopted charges the proper expense of superintendence to each machine as operated, and to idle shop capacity as machines are idle, by the simple use of the machine rate. It seems to me a perfectly satisfactory method of distributing an expense which it is a little difficult otherwise to deal with justly. I am indebted for it to two separate sources. The first is Mr. Hamilton Church's articles in the *Engineering Magazine,* to which I have alluded at some length; the second is the quite independent suggestion of a shop manager who was carefully considering the distribution of his machine costs.

Mr. Murdoch then comes to my " final stumbling block." It is manufactured out of queer materials, including the assumption that I proposed to capitalize the same expenditure twice, charge interest twice, depreciation twice, the same repair expenditure twice! And this in a system of accounts in which it is at least proposed that plant inventories, stock accounts, and costs, shall be balanced with the commercial books!

Under the heading " Interest on value of machines " Mr. Murdoch quotes me as saying that the inclusion of this in costs is a method of my own. Mr. Murdoch is curiously mistaken in

295

attributing the statement to me. If he will read the first of the series of articles of which he is criticising certain details he will find more than one plain statement to the contrary of what he represents me as saying.

Finally Mr. Murdoch objects to applying the depreciation percentage to diminishing values. The reasons for doing it are two. First, that while an old machine may do the same work as it did when it was new, the work is unlikely to be of the same value, because when a machine is new it is generally competing with older and less advantageously designed machines, and when it is old it is generally competing with newer and more advantageously designed machines. And second, if a machine as it grows older is maintained at its original efficiency it is by means of an increasing repair expense, and there is some hope of equalizing this by a diminishing depreciation charge, so that at least the operation of the old machine shall not enter into the cost of products with a higher machine charge than the operation of the same machine new. The argument would have the same force if we were not considering detailed costs, but only the general profit and loss account.

And as to the charge "too involved to be practicable," that is a matter best judged by actual test. If one actually does a thing and comes to know both cost and result, one is in a pretty fair position to decide what is worth while and what is not.

I may say in conclusion that I do not think Mr. Murdoch's criticism, or in consequence, this reply, has any but a slight bearing upon the articles criticised. In those articles I endeavored, with whatever success or failure, to work out a consistent scheme, the scope of which I indicated in the first of them. I have reason, as I have pointed out, to believe that Mr. Murdoch did not read the first article, and he did not wait for the last. Under the circumstances, his understanding of the matter criticised is necessarily limited, and his criticism practically one of isolated details.

Shoe Factory Cost Accounts

Shoe Factory Cost Accounts.*

By John Whitmore.

I do not know whether any of you will remember that when I talked here some evenings two years ago concerning machine shop cost accounts I said that I chose the cost accounts of machine shops as a convenient beginning to the general subject of manufacturing cost accounts. It is of course plain that the machinery industry occupies an initial position in modern manufacturing and there is a certain natural order in taking first the accounts of the industry in which the machinery is produced and then the accounts of the industries in which it is operated to give other products. There is, however, a second reason, having I believe a natural relationship to the first, in the fact that machine shop operations are characterized by largeness and directness, rather than by the complexity and minuteness which in varying degrees are found in many other industries. I do not mean that the machinery industry is itself simple. The largeness and directness I speak of come rather from a certain simplicity in the materials, and a rather considerable average duration of the processes.

The development of cost accounting must begin from simple methods and simple ideas and definitions. In the machinery manufacturing industry as a rule materials can be charged in their original form direct from the storehouse to the cost account for the finished product for which a manufacturing order is issued. And the machine processes, and the work of a single workman, are generally speaking of sufficient duration so that it is quite easy to record the time of beginning and the time of finishing in every case. A very large percentage of the work may be paid by the piece. These are conditions which make possible simple and direct methods in the cost accounts.

Then it is natural to begin with the idea of merely determining the cost of the respective products, that is, to state the cost of the products as they are in succession turned out. This is indeed very generally believed to be the sole purpose of cost accounts.

Later in the practice of cost accounting there have to be considered methods of dealing with less simple materials, handled and treated in the first place in quantities not yet divided up according to manufacturing orders for the product; and with numerous and small operations. And there have to be considered

* A lecture delivered before the New York University School of Commerce. Accounts and Finance, February 19th, 1908.

12

a!ternative definitions of cost, and uses of cost accounts going far beyond the mere stating of cost prices for the products.

It is for the purpose of illustrating such developments and of tracing their relation to the simpler forms of cost accounts that I have chosen the cost accounts of the shoe-manufacturing industry as the subject for my present talk to you.

I believe that the existing need in relation to the matter of cost accounting is that it be rendered more systematic. Hitherto it has not been this, whatever merits it may have had. There are principles which may not be violated, general methods which should be accepted as authoritative, lines of development which should be defined; but the student of cost accounting who seeks an explicit statement concerning these things will, I believe, at present not find it. Heretofore we have started out we will say to state the cost of the various products of a factory, and we have used such means as some experience or some faculty of invention have suggested, and without doubt valuable results have by these means been accomplished in individual work. But cost accounting is not systematized by these means, and the materials for the use of the student of cost accounting remain comparatively slight.

In the machinery manufacturing industry we have first the storehouse receiving materials at cost price and issuing them at cost price upon requisitions bearing manufacturing order numbers, with the consequent debits to the storehouse in the first place, and in the second credits to the storehouse and debits to the cost accounts for the respective manufacturing order numbers. Next we have machinists' time slips giving job numbers and the time worked on each job, with the consequent distribution of the pay-roll to the cost accounts. Next we have, amongst the fairly well established methods, the charge to the cost accounts and the credit to the shop expenses of hourly rates for the machine tools used. Then there is a distribution, upon whatever basis may in any case be found to be the fairest, of the remaining expenses of manufacture. What are the remaining expenses of manufacture and what are the rules, as far as there are established rules, for dealing with them? I would say that the remaining expenses of manufacture to be taken up in the cost accounts for product do not include (unless by a separate supplementary charge like the addition to factory cost to cover commercial expenses) the expense of all or any part of a factory being idle beyond a fair

83

allowance for lost time; and I would say that the expenses of a factory having two or more departments should not be generally distributed, but should as far as possible be divided between the departments, so that each department shall have its proper expense rate, and not merely the average expense rate of the whole factory.

Concerning the definition of cost I would say that true or correct cost does not necessarily include every expense incurred in the course of producing an article. Accidents and blunders occur and the cost, as in some instances the cost of unused factory capacity, may be so great that it would be absurd to state it as a part of the cost of the product. If this is established, it establishes the principle that improper costs may be separated and stated under a heading which will distinguish between these and manufacturing expenses properly and necessarily incurred. This principle is rather far reaching; its application may be of the greatest practical value; and it is susceptible of abuse. The danger is of assuming an impossibly perfect standard of working and of failing to allow for a certain unescapable average of accident and failure. Or again of applying in complex work the standards that are fair where work is simple, or in special work where new means of working to a new end have to be developed, the standards that are fair where processes are thoroughly established.

It is possible to carry the application of the principle of distinguishing between proper and improper costs so far as to use calculations of proper costs and then to direct the cost accounting to showing the variations of actual from calculated costs. This involves the setting up of complete standards for quality in materials and efficiency in working, and is not to be confused with estimates of probable cost which are arrived at by any superficial method, or except with the idea of continuously testing actual and calculated costs by each other.

Calculations of proper costs with provision in the accounting for showing the variations of actual from calculated costs constitute a plan which may be adopted for another reason than the one just dealt with. In some industries the manufacturing orders are so numerous that it is scarcely possible to have a separate cost account fully worked out for every order, while it is still quite practicable to have a calculation of cost for every article and to show where and how the calculated costs are varied from. I

14

could illustrate this to you by describing systems of cost accounts in the hard and soft rubber manufacturing industries and in the stationery manufacturing industry.

As to the purposes of cost accounts I would regard these as being three: 1. The bookkeeping purpose, which is to make a record, to state profits and losses, and to state the value of materials remaining in process of manufacture, otherwise only determined by inventory. 2. The economic purpose, which is to trace waste and by eliminating it to secure the lowest cost of production. 3. The commercial purpose, which is to ascertain the prices at which products can be sold profitably.

I desire, however, as I have said to talk to you to-night particularly about the cost accounts of the shoe manufacturing industry and in describing them to trace the relationship of the methods used to what I have concluded to regard as the basic method used in machine shop cost accounts.

Materials in the shoe manufacturing industry fall into four distinct divisions: 1, Upper Leathers; 2, Sole Leathers; 3, Linings; and 4, Miscellaneous Materials including what are called Findings. Upper leathers are, except for a possible small percentage of them, first sorted to grade them according to the standard requirements in the particular factory, inasmuch as it is not practicable for the manufacturers of upper leathers to sell them graded for the requirements of the individual shoe manufacturers. Sole leathers may be bought by the side or may be bought cut into outer soles, inner soles, etc., and heels may be bought manufactured. Where the sole leather products are bought manufactured it of course reduces the operations and simplifies the cost accounts, but as the leather is commonly bought in the side, it is necessary to consider it in that form. It has then to be cut up into outer soles, inner soles, and heel pieces, and the heels have to be manufactured. In large factories making the cheaper shoes in large quantities cotton linings may be cut in quantities for stock, in which case the linings department is a separate department, having its separate cost and stock accounts, which are of a simple character. In smaller factories making more expensive shoes the linings are cut for the individual order of shoes at the same time that the upper leathers are cut. Miscellaneous materials include various things, such as buttons, buckles, bows of ribbon, etc., which are or may be issued from the storehouse for the particular shoe orders; and in the same storehouse

15

there may be included the smaller findings, including needles and thread and paste, which are issued in reasonable quantities to the several departments requiring them, and must be distributed to the product as a part of the general expense of the departments severally. The location and the care of the minor materials may be governed by considerations peculiar to each factory. There will wherever cost accounts are kept be inevitably and at least three storehouses: one for upper leathers, and one for sole leathers, and one for miscellaneous materials and findings. Only the last of these three receives and issues its materials exactly as a machine shop storehouse receives and issues them, *i. e.*, receiving them at cost price and issuing them at the same cost price, either upon requisitions bearing the number of a manufacturing order for shoes, or upon a department requisition for supplies chargeable to the department expense account. The upper leather storeroom receives what from the shoe factory point of view are unsorted leathers, and issues sorted leathers. The sole leather storeroom receives sides of leather and cuts them up and issues the various products. It is obvious that these two are not storerooms in the simplest sense. It is proper to consider whether there is a departure from the principle of storeroom control in permitting materials to be worked upon and their form and their cost changed, without formal issue given its full effect not only in storeroom ledgers, but in the controlling stores accounts in the general ledger. I will take first the upper leather storeroom operations and records and describe them.

There is for the upper leather storeroom, as for every separate storeroom, a storeroom ledger controlled by an account in the general ledger under a corresponding title. As upper leathers are bought and received at the factory they are debited to accounts for the various kinds of leather in the storeroom ledger and they are by monthly totals charged to the general ledger controlling account for the upper leather storeroom. So far of course the procedure is exactly the same as it is with machine shop storehouses. There is immediately thereafter a difference. In the upper leather storeroom of a shoe factory they take the skins as they are received and sort them for the purpose I have already described. A single lot of skins as received has of course a single price per square foot. When the single lot is sorted into several grades there must necessarily be a new price for each of these grades. It is plain that there will possibly be something arbitrary

16

in these prices, that is they are not fixed by actual bargain between two parties. The first necessity is of course to establish distinctly what constitutes each of the grades that are to be produced by the sorting process,—that is to define as clearly as possible the standard of the quality of each. The next thing is to fix relatively fair prices for these different grades; that is to say, if the value of the highest grade is represented by 100, the value of the second grade we will say will be represented by 90, and the value of the third grade by 75. I am explaining that in the first place the matter to be determined is simply the relationship between the values attaching to the qualities represented by the different grades. They must in the first place be relatively fair to each other as far as it is possible for them to be made by the judgment of people expert in the business, and knowing the exact uses and values of the different grades for the purpose of making their own product. When this relationship is established, the next thing is to adopt a level at which these values will correspond to the existing market, and then the highest price may perhaps be 25 cents, and the next one 10 per cent. less than that, and the third 25 per cent. less than the first. When this is done, the concern is ready to sort its upper leathers as received, and price the products, and determine whether the particular lot of leather sorted is giving them a somewhat better or a somewhat worse result than the standard established for the existing market, and exactly by what percentage the result is better or worse. The sorting and its result are recorded on a form that is called a Sorting Report. On the debit side of the sorting report is put the quantity and the cost price of the leather sorted, and next the sorting labor, and next a charge to cover the general expenses of the storeroom in which the sorting is done, and this is very properly calculated at such a price per dozen as, according to the annual expenses of the department, and the number of dozens of skins annually handled, will suffice to take up these expenses. On the other side of the sorting report are stated the products of the sorting. Then the gain or loss is determined. Now the gain or loss that is shown by these means comes from one of two possible causes, supposing that in the first place the work of fixing the relative values of the grades of leather produced from sorting has been satisfactorily done. These two possible causes are: 1, That the level of prices in use is not in accordance with the market, that is, it is either too high or too low. If this is the case, it will of course be apparent

17

by there being continually a surplus or continually a deficiency shown in the sortings, and the indication would be that the level of prices needed to be raised or lowered. The second cause would be that the particular lot of leather was either an unusually good lot, or an unusually poor lot, and it may be stated that there is no such thing as absolute evenness in lots of leather. This is a condition that probably attaches to all materials in as nearly a natural state as are even skins which have gone through the manufacturing processes prior to their purchase by a shoe factory. If in the sortings the resulting surpluses or deficiencies are pretty equal, it proves that the level of the prices is all right, and that surplus or deficiency comes from the second cause stated, namely, the natural variation in the materials. And it may not be natural variation merely. One manufacturer may either constantly or occasionally be furnishing grades of leather that are below the average, the purchases from him being consequently disadvantageous; and another manufacturer may either constantly or occasionally be furnishing grades that are better than the average. The importance of bringing out these facts must be immediately apparent. One use of the accounts is to enable the shoe manufacturer to avoid disadvantageous buying through his immediate knowledge of the actual results obtained in sorting the various purchases. I will presently explain to you how this information is stated in a very simple and convenient form for use.

If now the sorting has resulted in an excess of credits over debits on the sorting report, then the figure necessary to complete the balance is placed on the debit side of the sorting report as a surplus, and its percentage upon the products of the sorting is calculated, so that we have in this case a surplus of say 1 per cent. or 2 per cent.; and if the sorting has resulted in an excess of debits over credits, the figure required to balance is placed on the credit side of the sorting report as a deficiency, and this is similarly calculated as a percentage on the products of the sorting, and is stated as a deficiency of say 1 per cent. or 2 per cent.

There is at this point a question which may be considered carefully. The actual cost of the products is in every case higher or lower by the percentage of surplus or deficiency, than the prices fixed for the different grades of leather. It is very simple to adjust these prices to actual cost by adding or deducting that percentage, and then, as far as the accounts go, the surplus or deficiency feature would disappear, and the prices placed on the

18

products of the sorting would have exactly absorbed the cost of those products. As one grade of leather is produced from many sortings, there would then be a stock of that leather consisting of a number of lots at different prices. This is not unlike a condition which will occur in any storehouse, and which I mentioned in connection with machine shop storehouses, namely, that there may at any time be a stock of materials which does not consist of a single purchase, and that the different purchases may be at different prices, the date of the purchases and the markets on those dates having been different. Under these circumstances and in the case of machine shop accounts, some people think it a good plan to exhaust the earliest purchase at its own price first, and then proceed to the later purchases at their respective prices. I have never done this, and I do not think that it is the best way. I think that the stock of the same goods is best treated at any time as a unit and its price averaged. I believe I stated my reasons for this fully when I was talking of the issues from machine shop storehouses.

Suppose now that in the case of sorted leathers, the prices put on products of the sorting should always be adjusted according to the percentage of surplus or deficiency, and these products should be carried into their respective accounts at these exact prices, and then in issuing these prices should be averaged in accordance with the practice that I described in connection with machine shop storehouses. We should probably come back in our issues to the standard prices put upon the different grades, or very close to them. This would in my opinion have two disadvantages. First, it would be considerable clerical labor with no corresponding gain; and second, while the result of averaging the different prices for the stock actually on hand would probably result in again approximating in the issues the standard prices first established for the grades, there would still be a variation which would be purely accidental, and which would be in the cost price of every finished shoe, and would need to be watched in connection with the cost prices of finished shoes for any significance that it might have in that connection. In other words, by this method there is clerical work created, and simplicity in the accounts is lost.

The other way of dealing with this matter, and the way that I believe is the best, is to carry the products of the sortings in stock and to issue them at the standard prices in use, and to

19

carry in a separate account the surpluses obtained on the sorting reports, and either on the other side of the same account or in still another account, the deficiencies similarly obtained. For it is to be borne in mind that as long as there is no change in the market that necessitates a change in the level of the prices put upon the products of sorting, the cost figures for shoes are based upon a known price for upper leathers, and the same is true as will presently be seen in regard to sole leathers. Under the circumstances the use of the cost figures is both simpler and safer than if every cost price depended upon whether the particular lot of upper leather used had sorted advantageously, or the particular lot of sole leather had cut up advantageously.

I will now review the procedure in regard to this matter and carry it a little further. Upper leathers having been received in stock, they are, as quickly as possible thereafter, sorted. Either the whole of the lot of leather or any part of it may be taken for sorting. Whatever is taken is entered on the debit side of a sorting report, and in due course the expenses attaching to those leathers in the storeroom, which is also the sorting room, are added on the debit side. On the credit side are stated the products of the sorting at standard prices, which are calculated to be relatively fair to each other according to the qualities of the products, and are calculated to be on such a level that for all purchases on a given market they will as closely as possible take up the actual cost. Then the surplus or deficiency is filled in as I have described. The products of the sorting are then placed in stock as graded leathers ready to issue for shoe making purposes. The sorting report is then taken by the clerk keeping the storeroom ledger, and everything on the debit side is posted to the credit of the proper accounts, that is, to the credit of the accounts to which the leather when it was purchased and received was debited, and to the credit of the sorting labor account, and to the credit of general expense account, and to the credit of surplus account. And everything on the credit side is posted to the debit of the proper accounts, that is, the products of the sorting are posted to the debit of the accounts for the grades of leather produced, and the deficiency is posted to the debit of the deficiency account. It will be seen that this leaves the ledger in balance. No entry whatever is made in the general books in connection with this sorting operation.

In the accounts in the storehouse ledger for the products of

20

sorting there are between the debit and the credit sides of the account two columns, the first headed " surplus " and the second "deficiency," and when the products are posted from the sorting reports to the debit of these accounts, the percentage of surplus or deficiency on the sorting report is entered in one of these columns. It will now be seen that reference to these accounts will show all the variations in the cost of obtaining a given grade of leather throughout a period of time. There can be very quickly seen for a considerable period where the highest cost has been, and where the lowest cost has been; and whether the shipments of a single manufacturer are of even quality; whether they are steadily of high quality, or steadily of low quality, or variable. This is information of the utmost value to the buyer and it is here, in the ordinary course of the bookkeeping, stated in its most concise and clear form.

Proceeding now to the general ledger in order to complete the description of the bookkeeping routine in regard to the upper leather storeroom. The upper leather storeroom controlling account in the general ledger will be conveniently divided into four, the four accounts being ultimately closed into one. To the first will be charged all purchases of upper leathers; to the second will be charged the pay-roll of the storeroom; to the third, all sundry expenses of the storeroom; and to the fourth will be credited the issues of leather from storeroom to factory. This group of accounts will control and will be in agreement with the upper leather storeroom ledger. It follows that the pay-roll and general expense items will be brought into the storeroom ledger. It will now be seen that the credits of labor posted from the sorting reports are, in the storeroom ledger, set against the actual pay-rolls; and the credits of general expenses posted from sorting reports are set against the debits of actual general expenses incurred; and that the storehouse ledger covers the receipt of upper leathers at the purchase prices, the handling and sorting operations at their cost, and the storage and issue of the products of sorting; and that the general ledger controlling account divided into four sections—1st, materials; 2d, labor; 3d, general expense; and 4th, issues of leather, is kept in agreement with the storehouse ledger which it controls. The issues are made in the ordinary storeroom way, upon requisitions for leather to manufacture the shoes covered by a shoe manufacturing order. In shoe factory language, they are issued in accordance with the

21

cutting slips for the lots of shoes for which orders have been placed in the factory. The cutting slips are posted to the credit of the accounts in the storeroom ledger, and they are summarized for credit to the controlling account in the general ledger, and postings can be made direct from the cutting slips to the cost accounts.

There is of course here a great variation from the routine and the form of the records in machine shop storehouses, but I believe it is merely a variation in practice to conform to operations following a different course, and not a departure from the principle which governs the organization and records of machine shop storehouses. To illustrate this we may suppose that a machine shop storehouse might have in it the machinery necessary for cutting bar iron and steel. If it were convenient to do this there could be no objection upon principle to its being done. Even in this slight operation we have something essentially similar to the sorting of upper leathers in the upper leather storeroom of a shoe factory. I want to make it plain that in different industries cost accounts rest upon the same principles, and, in spite of great apparent differences, have still the same methods fundamentally.

In the case of the sole leather storeroom, a step is taken that goes further than the sorting process in the upper leather storeroom, that is to say, the sides of leather are cut up and outer soles, and inner soles, and heel pieces, are obtained. As far as the records are concerned, the procedure is the same. Instead of a sorting report, we have the cutting report. On the debit side of the cutting report is entered at its cost price the leather that is taken to cut up, and the cutting labor is entered, and a percentage upon the cutting labor to take up the general expenses of the room; and on the credit side of the cutting report are entered the products, outer soles, and inner soles, and heel pieces, and scrap leather. These products are priced in a manner that is parallel to the pricing of the products of the sorting of the upper leathers, that is to say, relatively fair prices are established for the different products, and these are adjusted to a level at which they are calculated to take up the actual costs; and then there is, just as in the other case, a percentage of surplus or deficiency. As a storeroom operation, the outer and inner soles are merely cut out in their first shape. The further operations upon the soles are sometimes actually done in the same room, but constructively they are done subsequent to their issue from the storeroom. The heels

22

on the other hand are actually manufactured for stock, and these manufacturing operations may be treated as storeroom operations, in which case the heel making report belongs for bookkeeping purposes exclusively to the sole leather storeroom. In the general ledger the controlling account for the sole leather storeroom will be in four divisions, for materials purchased, and labor, and general expenses, and issues of leather, just as in the case of the upper leather storeroom controlling account. And in the sole leather storeroom the cutting reports and heel making reports, with their surpluses and deficiencies, will be posted to the sole leather storeroom ledger in exactly the same manner as in the case of the upper leather storeroom. The issues from the sole leather storeroom are also made at the standard prices in use.

The amount of net surplus or net deficiency in the upper leather storeroom should be stated week by week, and the standard of prices raised or lowered at any time that it is seen to be necessary in order to keep the prices placed on the products of the sorting, and used in issuing the sorted leathers, in substantial agreement with actual costs. They should be kept so adjusted as to leave a little surplus, which is very likely to be needed at the end of the fiscal period to take care of some depreciation which may take place in some stocks. The surpluses and deficiencies in the sole leather storeroom should be watched week by week in exactly the same manner, and the standard prices on the products there should be kept adjusted in just the same way for the same purpose of keeping a surplus, but not an excessive one, to provide for needs which develop in one shape or another. The small surplus to be kept in each of these two cases is merely a proper margin of safety.

You will remember that I said that in machine shop operations, the individual operations are of sufficient length so that the time taken by each can be easily recorded, and the individual labor charge for each operation, and the individual machine charge for each operation, can be posted to the cost account for the job. It would be exceedingly laborious to do this in shoe factory cost accounts. As far as the labor charges go, it is possible to do it in shoe factories of moderate size, and it is done. Presumably, the labor of doing it in large shoe factories would be merely proportionate to their volume of operations, but it would for many reasons be not merely expensive, but difficult to maintain at the

23

requisite standard of accuracy. It would seem therefore that as a general proposition there has got to be some variation or adaptation of the procedure in machine shop cost accounts in order to satisfactorily effect the labor and machine charges in shoe factory cost accounts. In regard to the labor I have used what I have called "Labor Cost Sheets," that is, for each kind of shoe made, a series of cost sheets corresponding to the different departments through which the shoe goes. For a single kind of shoe, there would be labor cost sheets for the sole leather department covering all operations subsequent to the original storeroom operation of cutting the soles out, for the upper leather cutting, for the stitching room, the assembling room, and the finishing room. On each of these cost sheets is specified the series of operations performed in the particular room on the particular kind of shoe, and on each there are two columns for the prices, the first being for piece prices which are fixed, and the second being for day work pieces, which are calculated upon the day wage and the average day's work for the respective operations. These labor cost sheets can be prepared according to what is called the sample shoe. In actual ordering, customers frequently vary the sample shoe. Where these variations involve changed labor expense, it is very necessary in order to protect profits, that they be very carefully watched, and the difference in the cost that is created clearly seen. Where these differences occur, the standard labor cost sheets have to be modified accordingly, for the purpose of the cost accounts for such shoes.

To use labor cost sheets in the manner described is of course an immense saving of labor as compared with the individual posting to cost sheets of a charge for each separate operation. Where every operation that is credited to a workman is posted to a cost sheet, the complete distribution of the pay-roll is assured in a manner that is not accomplished in the first place by the use of labor cost sheets. The check upon the pay-roll, and upon its distribution in the cost accounts, has however to be obtained in some way, and the way adopted is this: The pay-rolls are analyzed, as they should be in any case and even regardless of cost accounts, first as between departments, and next as between piece labor, and productive day labor; and ledger accounts for these divisions of the pay-roll are set up either in the general ledger, or in a subsidiary manufacturing ledger, according to the volume of the

24

operations and the way the bookkeeping is arranged. This gives us one side of the figures that we want to compare. In the next place, an analytical summary is made of all the cost sheets for the product, that is to say, the sheet upon which the cost sheets are summarized has a considerable number of columns, including columns for the piece work and the productive day work in each of the departments. The cost sheets, which are summarized weekly or monthly, are further summarized on a similar form for the season; and so it will be seen that the totals of, for instance, the stitching room piece labor, and the stitching room productive day labor, as taken up in the cost accounts by means of the labor cost sheets, are arrived at, and are available for comparison with the corresponding figures accumulated in the ledger accounts from the analysis of the succeeding weekly pay-rolls throughout the season.

Now while I have not as yet done it in any case, I am satisfied that something parallel to this can be accomplished in relation to the machinery charges. If in the first place, the annual cost of each machine is determined, as in the case of machine tools in a machine shop, the annual expense can be reduced to a daily expense, and a fair daily output for each machine can be calculated, and a price can be put upon each operation, that is, a machine rate for each operation exactly as there is a labor price for each operation. The labor cost sheet could then be made into a labor and machine expense cost sheet, and against each operation would be put not only the piece price, or the calculated day-labor cost, but in an additional column the calculated machine rate for the operation; and these machinery charges would be summarized in the same way that labor taken up in the cost accounts is summarized, and would be credited against the actual machinery expenses in the various departments, exactly as is done with the machine rates taken up in machine shop cost accounts.

In a single hour it is of course not possible to talk very fully or very descriptively concerning the cost accounts of an important industry. I have tried to outline the cost accounts of the shoe manufacturing industry, and to show where the methods of cost accounting in this industry must vary from the methods that I have described in the machinery manufacturing industry, and at the same time to show that there is throughout a distinct and intelligible relationship between the two.

25

Some Cost Accounting Terms

Some Cost Accounting Terms

AN INTRODUCTION TO A DISCUSSION OF THE NATURE AND USES OF FACTORY ACCOUNTS

By John Whitmore

When names seem expressive, but are not accurately so, there is a danger that they may govern our conceptions of the things named, and if these are still in process of development, names may even determine their eventual character. It seems to me that this is what has happened, and is still happening, to what we have all of us called "cost accounts." The name is simple and striking. It seems to convey a meaning perfectly, and even to constitute a binding definition. It is but natural if after a while cost accounts are found to have been fitted to their name; cost accounts are accounts to determine costs.

The federal trade commission has probably been one of the principal influences which have furthered among manufacturers a sense of the necessity of cost accounts, but always as far as I know to the end that they may have knowledge of the costs of their products. And a recent and not unauthoritative definition of cost accounts speaks of their sole purpose as being to state the costs of products. Nor, notwithstanding the emphasis laid constantly by practitioners of cost accounting upon the potential uses of cost accounts in attaining economy of manufacture, can one doubt that such a definition of cost accounts, as actually existing, has a wide, though of course not a universal, accuracy.

Now cost accounts originally bore another name. They were called "factory accounts." Apparently someone with an instinct for the striking word, managed to change their name, I believe with unfortunate results. The new name of "cost accounts," truly understood, is perfectly comprehensive, for all the expenses of manufacturing, from the building of a manufacturing plant to finishing the products for the market, are nothing but the costs of such products (unless, indeed, they are waste), and they are none of them ever recoverable at all except as they are recovered in the sale of the products.

But unfortunately the term "cost accounts" was liable to a narrower interpretation, and this is what has befallen it. They

193

became a separate and limited thing, outside of the main system of double-entry bookkeeping and for the sole purpose of arriving at cost figures.

In the year 1887 there was published a book which was for long, and I am inclined to think that it still is, the best existing book on the subject of manufacturing cost accounts. But it was not called cost accounts, nor do I think that term occurs in the whole course of it. It was written by Emil Garcke, managing director of the British Electric Traction Company, and J. M. Fells, general manager of the Salt Union, Limited. They appear to have been important industrial executives, and they were certainly accomplished accountants. The title of the book was *Factory Accounts*, and in it there was never the idea that the factory accounts were anything other than an integral part of the total system of double-entry accounting, or that they were for a single purpose, or for any limited number of specified purposes, for their many uses are considered step by step throughout the description of them. Contrast with the idea that cost accounts are for the single purpose of ascertaining costs of products even the following uses of factory accounts which are more specially dwelt upon in this book published as long ago as 1887:

    (a) To give (of course) the cost of production, both by completed products and in detail;

    (b) To disclose wastes and to point the ways to lowering costs;

    (c) To account for materials as cash is accounted for, and to regulate them in accordance with the factory needs;

    (d) To give continuous inventory figures, making frequent profit and balance-sheet statements possible;

    (e) To create a moral effect upon the employees, both by their knowledge of the existence of a strict accounting and by their own participation in effecting it;

    (f) To furnish a sound basis for participation by employees in profits arising from increased efficiency, binding the interests of employer and workmen more closely together.

It is possible that if we had held to the idea of factory accounts as an integral part of the balanced double-entry accounts of a manufacturer, with their unbroken chain of controlling accounts and controlled books, and had not substituted a narrower idea of "cost accounts," it might have been better. I think factory accounts is a more accurate and more useful term than cost accounts.

The next cost accounting term that I will consider is "tying in," applied to the effecting of an agreement between the figures in the cost accounts and corresponding figures in the general books. A recent important publication,* in reviewing the history of cost accounting in the United States, says "the first long step forward of progress in overhead accounting came with the appreciation that costs should be tied in with the general books."

Now "tying in" can not possibly be anything more, and I do not see how it can be anything less, than bringing the cost accounts within the double-entry system of the general accounts. As I have already said, in Garcke & Fells' book published in 1887 there is not the slightest suggestion that they shall be outside of that system, with the inevitable consequence of being unbalanced and uncontrolled. They are included in it by the simplest means. The general ledger stores account controls the materials and supplies ledgers. The manufacturing account controls the cost ledgers. The stock account controls the finished-stock ledgers. The bookkeeping principle, one might almost say the procedure, is identical with that of the controlling account and controlled ledger for accounts receivable. The "tying in" is just the same in the one case as the other, and it is nothing but simple double-entry bookkeeping. If factory bookkeeping is double-entry bookkeeping, there can be no need to talk of tying in. The cost accounts will be tied in already, quite perfectly.

And then there is the unfortunate term "overhead." This came into use but a very limited number of years ago, and seemed almost immediately to achieve a universal popularity. At present, practically, one is forced to use the term, however one rebels against it. In the original *Century Dictionary*, published about forty years ago, there was no such word in the present sense. In the *Supplement*, published about twenty years later, it appeared, defined as "average; applicable to all." Costs were then, and have been ever since, down to this very day, defined as consisting of materials, direct labor and overhead. In the pamphlet issued by the department of manufacture of the Chamber of Commerce of the United States, already referred to, it is said:

> "Overhead is usually defined in accounting text books to include the elements of cost that are left over after charging direct to a product the readily allocated materials and the labor that have been employed direct in its manufacture.

* *The Evolution of Overhead Accounting:* Department of manufacture, Chamber of Commerce of the United States.

195

. . . Indirect items of cost include such things as the super-intendent's salary, power, light, the cost of owning and oper-ating buildings and machinery, and so on. Overhead is the general term applied to these indirect costs."

The Chamber of Commerce pamphlet describes how at first all this "overhead" was distributed to the different products on the basis of direct labor, money or hours, without departmentalizing expenses; how later came the departmentalization of expenses; and later still machine rates.

So far I believe it is plain that what is being considered is the machine industries. Indeed, I believe this is true of nearly all discussions of cost accounting, even to this day. As long as we assume this limitation, the methods of cost accounting advocated are intelligible, and all of them probably are still useful under the different conditions in the machine industries today. But there are other and vast industries to which such procedure seems to have little relation and often no relation whatsoever. In the paper manufacturing industries there can be no distribution of other expenses on the basis of direct labor, for labor and all other expenses of the principal part of the mill must be charged accord-ing to paper-machine time, and though this may seem virtually a machine rate it has little or no likeness to machine rates de-termined separately, and with much detailed distribution, to each of, perhaps, a hundred machines in a machine shop. In foundries the distribution on the basis of direct labor has a limited place and is effected with necessary modifications. In the large forging operations, it is true, there are hammer and press rates which are practically identical in character with machine-tool rates. In the metallurgical and chemical industries the procedure is quite special to the operations, and has no likeness whatever to the procedure in the mechanical industries.

On the other hand I believe the distribution and division of all expenses to "production centres" may be accepted as a universal principle, for the production centre may be the total of a factory, or a department of a factory, or a process, or a single machine, a single forging hammer or press, a single furnace of any character, a single still (as in oil refining), a single kettle (as in soap manufac-turing), a group of tanks (as in electrolytic copper refining), or in fact any unit or group of units in any industrial processes.

But not all "overhead" is expense of production. Commonly a part of it, and often a considerable part, is expense of idleness.

196

Some little time after the publication of Hamilton Church's *Proper Distribution of the Expense Burden,** I talked on a few evenings to the students at the New York University School of Commerce and Accounts, and in those talks I dwelt long upon the importance of Mr. Church's book. But I dissented altogether from his supplementary rate by which he brought all factory expenses whatsoever into the cost of goods produced. I pointed out the imperative need of separating the expenses of what I then called "idle factory capacity," but which the present Chamber of Commerce pamphlet, contending for exactly the same thing, calls by the more convenient term of "idle facilities." The substance of what I said then was later printed as a series of articles in THE JOURNAL OF ACCOUNTANCY in the months of August, 1906, to January, 1907. This series of articles was reprinted in full in *The Accountant*, the organ of the Institute of Chartered Accountants in England and Wales, November, 1906, to February, 1907.†

"Overhead," therefore, defined as "average; applicable to all," is in large part expenses of individual production centres, costs of single processes and even of single products, as direct in their ultimate determination as the expense of materials and direct labor; and it is in varying but considerable part expense of idle facilities, and no part of the costs of any products at all. If it is doubted that the use of this word creates confused thinking, I may relate one trivial incident.

A few years ago I told a manufacturer, to whom I was talking of certain cost accounting plans as their development proceeded, that I proposed to distribute the purely general expenses of the machine shops on the basis of the combined machine rates and direct labor. He answered that it seemed to him that this would violate what he understood was "one of the first principles of cost accounting, that one must never distribute overhead on overhead." If he had used words of plain meaning and had said "You propose to distribute the purely general expenses of a machine shop on the combined cost of machine labor and men's labor," I do not think he would have gone on to the same conclusion. But instead of simple facts and actual relationships he was considering "overhead."

————

* This was originally a series of articles published in the *Engineering Magazine*, July to December, 1901.

† I see that there is a belief prevalent now that the necessity of excluding the cost of idle facilities from the cost of products, and making it a separate charge to profit and loss, was first perceived many years later (see page 1228 *Proceedings International Congress 1929*). That this is completely an error may be readily seen by reference to the articles in THE JOURNAL OF ACCOUNTANCY in the months and years above mentioned.—J. W.

197

The term "burden" is used now in the same sense as "overhead." They are used as absolute synonyms. All the time one comes across the expression "overhead or burden." Burden is at least a legitimate noun and consequently does not give one an immediate sense of bewilderment. In this connection it has also a different history. It originated in a period that is past, when expenses other than materials and direct labor were relatively small. Such was the state of affairs when Garcke & Fells' *Factory Accounts* was written in 1887. It is stated therein that many manufacturers were content to take out "prime cost" i. e. materials and direct labor, feeling that they could always make due allowance for the other expenses of manufacturing, without formal calculation. But "burden" and "overhead" live on together as alternative designations for the third element of cost in the machine industries. The limitation to the machine industries is my own, for it seems to me that such a limitation always exists without ever being mentioned.

I leave "overhead" and consider "burden," which is a word having a meaning that can be discussed. Is it truly expressive of the expenses of manufacturing other than labor? I believe that in many machine operations the labor might more correctly be called burden, than the power and tools by which the work is actually performed. In such operations how plain it is that the elements of cost are at least five:

> Materials,
> Direct labor,
> Power,
> Tools,
> General manufacturing expense.

If these five divisions were recognized, if they had passed into the common cost-accounting speech, instead of the single paper *Accounting for Burden* in the recent international congress, we might have had at least a paper on power cost accounts and a paper on machine rates.

Then there is the word "depreciation." For what this word represents of the constant contention of accountants through the years when necessary depreciation charges were so commonly resisted, I have a great respect. Nevertheless the term is inexact, and consequently it has been a mischief-maker. Often it was difficult or impossible to contend that physical depreciation had occurred, and, even if obsolescence were considered, probably

198

nothing of the kind was in sight. I believe the error was a fundamental error in the view taken of manufacturing plant. It was, and I believe often is, regarded as something having an actual value in itself, whereas its only value is in its use for production. Its creation is merely the first step, the initial process, in producing marketable goods, and the proportionate cost of that initial process is as much a part of the cost of every item of the resulting production as is the cost of any later process. It would seem impossible that there could at any time have been any question that all manufacturing plant has a limited life (whether limited by its being worn out or its being superseded) and that at the end of its life its cost has been a part of the cost of all the product obtained by its use, without excepting a single item of such product, from first to last; and that consequently by a process of amortization the cost of plant must be steadily absorbed into the cost of products, and that depreciation as a fact at any given time has nothing to do with the matter. I think amortization would always have been a better word.

There is another cost-accounting term that has come into use and that seems not unlikely to achieve a popularity like that of "overhead," and this is "pre-determined costs." Pre-determined costs have been put forward as something infinitely superior to actual recorded costs. I think myself that, whatever is meant by pre-determined costs, they can not but be something so absolutely different and distinct from costs actually recorded that the two are not comparable and that there can not be superiority of one over the other. "Pre-determined costs" are presumably comparable with any other estimates, or calculations, or forecastings of costs, before actual production, and I am not questioning any claims that may be made as to their uses and values, but I do not like the term. The *Century Dictionary* gives certain varied definitions of the word pre-determine, supporting each with quotations, and, in all except one, it is not man that pre-determines, but quite another Being. The single exception is represented by a quotation from Sterne's *Sentimental Journey:* "The moment I cast my eyes upon him, I was pre-determined not to give him a single sou." Which is of course quite a different thing from pre-determining the costs of manufacture.

Concerning estimates (which is all they can be) prior to manufacture, and costs actually recorded from day to day as the manufacturing progresses, and the uses of these two sets of figures in

199

conjunction with each other, it would be difficult to-day to add anything of real significance to the following quotations from Garcke & Fells' book published in 1887, although one speaker at the international congress seemed to think that before 1908 there were only the dark ages.

"Before any order to manufacture is given it is advisable, as tending to produce greater economy in cost of production, that the designer, draughtsman, or other person best acquainted with its processes and details, should, on a properly ruled and headed form, estimate the probable cost to be incurred in wages and materials in the production of the articles in question.   This estimate should be a minimum rather than a maximum one.   The works manager or foreman should be supplied with a complete specification of all material and parts included in the estimate.   The storekeeper should also be furnished with the same particulars, and should not without special authority issue more material for the order than is estimated."

"To ensure consideration of the question of what economies are practicable in construction or manufacture, the heads of the designing and manufacturing departments should be advised of the cost of each order when it is completed in such detail as permits of a comparison being instituted between the actual and estimated cost.   As a matter of convenience the estimate forms may include columns for the actual costs to be inserted when known.   The employer should be advised of the differences between actual and estimated costs in such detail as he may require.   It is also desirable that a comparative cost register should be compiled showing the difference in cost of making the same or similar articles under differing conditions of time, material, parts, or quantities.   This register will be specially serviceable in preparing estimates and quoting for orders, and permits of the necessary adjustments in quotations consequent upon the increase or decrease in the market price of material."

How simple the words, how temperate the phrasing throughout, and still I doubt whether there is any other book on factory accounts, even after this interval of 43 years, that can be read with so much profit to-day.

––––––

[My quotations from Messrs. Garcke & Fells' book are taken from the edition of 1902.   I think I can say from memory that this 1902 edition is substantially the same as the original edition of 1887.—J. W.]

200

Poverty and Riches of "Standard Costs"

Poverty and Riches of "Standard Costs"

By John Whitmore

"Standard costs" as used in the title of this article (and as used in the article itself wherever it is so written) means the system which is called by that name in the papers and discussions of the cost accounting division of the International Congress on Accounting, New York, 1929. This system includes the principle of ordinary standard costs, which is as old as organized manufacturing; and it includes the principle of measuring the variations of actual costs from standards; and it definitely, and as a matter of principle, and without distinction between industries of different characters, excludes the recording of costs as actually and directly incurred under each separate manufacturing or construction order; and it includes the using of standard costs as a basis for calculating additional remuneration to factory employees.

I have called this article "Poverty and riches of standard costs." What I regard as the poverty of the system is its so nearly exclusive emphasis on the calculation of costs before manufacture, at the expense of the character of the actual subsequent accounting, as is shown in its exclusion of manufacturing-order cost accounts even under conditions that render them most useful and valuable; and again in its throwing expenses of the most various characters together and distributing them all as "burden"; and again in its restriction to a single type of factory accounting, as if all manufacturing operations were of a single type. And what I regard as its riches is that from the same emphasis on the prior calculation of costs, there has emerged a plan for supplementing wages (completing the remuneration of factory labor) which substitutes a profound common interest, both in the operations as human labor and achievement, and in their financial results, for the narrow individual interests created or accentuated by most if not all existing supplementary wage schemes.

Throughout these articles and discussions there is constantly proclaimed the opposition (very largely imagined) of two systems of cost accounting, namely, the calculating of the costs of products before they are manufactured, and the accounting for the expenditures in the actual manufacturing under individual manufacturing order numbers. This is all indicated in a quotation

9

(*Proceedings of 1929 International Congress*, p. 863) from an article published in December, 1908, referred to as the beginning of the "standard costs" system, as follows:

> "There are two radically different methods of ascertaining costs; the first method, to ascertain them after the work is completed; the second method, to ascertain them before the work is undertaken. The first method is the old one. . . . The objection to the old method is not only that it delays information until little value is left in it, but that it is wholly and absolutely incorrect. . . ."

I commented in my article, published in the September, 1930, issue of THE JOURNAL OF ACCOUNTANCY, upon the curious belief, equally conspicuous in the foregoing quotation and in the papers and discussions of the 1929 international congress, that where individual cost accounts for manufacturing or construction orders are kept, there are no calculations of costs beforehand; and this is proclaimed as the blind omission of accountants, who were "like Lot's wife, everlastingly looking behind" (*Proceedings*, p. 1250). In some industries (within my own knowledge, the textile and paper-making industries are examples) accountants may calculate costs beforehand, from specifications of the products to be made and the materials to be used, and with existing manufacturing records. But in the engineering and machine shop industries? The work of estimating must be at least under the control of qualified engineers, and it requires the coöperation of the heads of the manufacturing departments and the departments auxiliary to the manufacturing departments: of foundries as to pattern and moulding and cleaning costs and risks of defectives; of machine shops as to the machining processes and often as to the economy of designing and making special tools; and so on as to any other works departments whose processes are not merely routine, but may be modified and adapted to special ends with varying costs, concerning which those who are closest to the operations must have the surest knowledge. If the work was ever omitted, it was not the omission of accountants, for it never was and never will be their work; and further it never was omitted, but was always done by the proper people. Any idea to the contrary is completely exploded by the passage quoted at the end of my article in this JOURNAL for September, from Garcke & Fells' *Factory Accounts* published in 1887 and always a standard work in this country.

10

The same quotation refutes also the idea expressed in such passages as the following:

> "The old methods of comparing actual costs with past actual costs have the element of almost entire uselessness" (*Proceedings*, p. 774).
>
> "Comparison of the cost of a part manufactured this month with its cost last month and the month before" (*Proceedings*, p. 867).

For though such comparisons are provided and tabulated quite automatically by the successive debits to the particular account in the stores ledgers, and though that comparison has the value of one strong light, amongst others, upon the state of manufacturing economy in the plant, the 1887 quotation describes the systematic procedure for showing the comparison between actual costs and costs previously estimated.

It must be borne in mind that the keeping of separate cost accounts for individual manufacturing orders is a method which belongs to the machine industries; and even in these, only where the manufacturing orders are usually large. Even so, it was at the time the 1908 article was published used only to a very moderate extent. In 1916, eight years later, the federal trade commission had reached the conclusion that not more than ten per cent. of American manufacturers knew the costs of their products. Some of these were keeping individual manufacturing-order cost accounts; and some were merely crediting their manufacturing accounts with the production at costs calculated beforehand; and some were using standard cost sheets, pure and simple, without bringing the figures into their general account books at all. I was familiar with all these procedures, and with others, in actual operation before December, 1908. In an article in this JOURNAL for May, 1908, I described the procedure in using standard costs to credit the manufacturing accounts in industries where the manufacturing orders are too small and numerous to permit the keeping of individual cost accounts for them, and at the same time I described the procedure in determining variances from standards in such industries.

The only fundamental difference between "the new method" and methods previously existing was that "the new method" excluded entirely the keeping of individual manufacturing-order cost accounts in any circumstances whatsoever. There was

11

otherwise, as I have already said, a difference in emphasis, not without important consequences.

"The new method," the "standard costs" system, has in the meantime developed its own character, indicated or described in the papers and discussions of the 1929 international congress. I proceed now to consider the "standard costs" system as so developed, and afterwards I will endeavor to indicate briefly what factory accounting which includes individual manufacturing-order cost accounts really is.

There is in the *Proceedings* only one article which describes the operation of the "standard costs" system in such a way that one can attempt to follow the working step by step, viz. Mr. Eric Camman's "Standard Costs: Installation and Procedure." For this reason alone I take it for consecutive examination, but before I conclude I shall quote important passages from the other articles, all written by stanch advocates of the "standard costs" system.

Mr. G. Charter Harrison has indicated the "standard costs" procedure briefly and rather casually on page 862 where he says that it "provides for showing on the debit side the actual expenditure and on the credit side the amount which should have been expended." Mr. Camman on page 876 outlines three alternative methods of debiting and crediting work-in-process accounts:

(a) to charge at actual costs and credit at standard costs. (This is apparently Mr. G. Charter Harrison's method.)
(b) to charge at standard and credit at standard—diverting differences to variance accounts.
(c) to charge at actual costs and credit at actual costs— inserting standard costs on both sides in parallel columns.

Mr. Camman dismisses method (a) as inadequate because it "allows cost variations to be concealed until a count of the work-in-process on hand is made." It is, however, worth noting that this method of charging work-in-process with the actual costs of manufacture, and then crediting the factory output at calculated costs (no individual manufacturing order cost accounts being kept) is a simple and within its own limits a useful method. I was familiar with it in two important (then and now) manufacturing corporations more than twenty-five years ago. It is of course true that the difference between actual and calculated costs is not shown until an inventory has been taken.

12

Under method (b) differences are diverted to variance accounts. How the differences are ascertained is not made very clear, but it is without waiting for a count of work-in-process, for it is said that methods (b) and (c), unlike (a) "disclose the differences and deal with them more promptly." It is indicated that practically the only difference between (b) and (c) is that under the former, the differences being diverted, the goods are charged to cost of goods sold at standard costs, while under the latter they are charged to cost of goods sold at actual costs. Mr. Camman prefers method (c).

We may proceed then to method (c) which is to charge work-in-process accounts at actual costs and credit at actual costs, inserting standard costs on both sides of the account in parallel columns. What this means is best expressed in Mr. Camman's own words (p. 878):

> "Costs of goods sold are expressed in actual costs. Inventories are carried at actual costs. The standard costs are confined to the factory ledgers and are not used in the balance-sheet, profit and loss account or other financial statements."

Now parallel columns are for comparison and the proposal must be to insert standard costs against comparable actual costs. How are the actual costs, against which comparable standard costs are to be inserted in parallel columns, ascertained? So far we know only that it shall not involve waiting for a count of work-in-process, but shall be accomplished "more promptly." As far as Mr. Camman explains, it is best to quote him (pp. 884 and 885):

> "The accounts are classified and grouped, the best grouping being by product classes. Under this arrangement a division is composed of similar products, the variations on which are likely to be similar in proportion and attributable to the same causes. Another arrangement is a grouping by departments and sub-departments; usually this plan requires more care and necessitates the devising of ingenious means to prevent the errors of excessive averaging which may result from too broad a combination.
>
> "It must be remembered that the variances which occur and which are reflected in the entries on the debit side of the accounts are averaged and spread over the cost of deliveries of products as reflected by the entries on the credit side of the accounts. Under a proper classification this method will give a reasonably correct result."

13

It is not very clear. But I will leave it where Mr. Camman leaves it. Differences are determined by product classes and are spread over the cost of deliveries of the products of each respective class, and with a proper classification a reasonably correct result is obtained, and the differences are ascertained more promptly than by waiting for a count of work-in-process. That is, they are presumably determined at not infrequent intervals. It would not be difficult to enumerate the possible ways in which this can be done, for their number is quite limited. I will, however, not stop to do this, for it would not with certainty identify Mr. Camman's method, and while I am concerned somewhat with the method I am more concerned with what is in the end accomplished. Concerning this I again quote Mr. Camman (p. 879):

> "The general purpose is to make suitable provision for the development of the figures in a manner which will be of practical help in the solution of the problems of management. It is in this direction that standard cost accounting is so much more adequate for modern industrial requirements than the job-order and unit-cost methods which it replaces."

Mr. Camman's conclusion is a statement and certain analyses of the "labor cost variance," the "burden cost variance," and the "material cost variance" for a period. These are spoken of as "some of the typical cost data which will be forthcoming through this method" (p. 885). I will in each instance give Mr. Camman's opening explanation of the source of the figures, and then his concluding statement of the results reached, each as nearly as possible in his own words. I must of course omit his detailed description of these analyses, but these can be read in the *Proceedings*.

Labor Cost Variance

> "The actual payroll is the source of information as to the amounts earned by direct labor workers during a period. The corresponding standard direct labor is derived by pricing and extending reports of production". (p. 885).
>
> "The pertinent facts as to labor have now been resolved: viz., 133% in hours at 105% in wages cause the labor cost ratio to be 140." (p. 886.)

Burden Cost Variance

> "Departmental burden accounts are the source of data as to the actual charges and accruals for indirect costs. The corresponding standard burden is figured by pricing and extending reports of production". (p. 887)

14

Actual machine hours were 77% of capacity and 103.1 of the standard hours for the actual production.

Standard burden for capacity............	$18,000.00
" " " actual production.....	13,440.00
" " " machine hours actually operated. (77% of capacity and 103.1 of standard hours for the production).....	13,860.00
Actual burden charges and accruals, per departmental burden accounts...........	11,970.00

Actual burden was therefore 89.1 of the standard for the production, and 86.4 of the standard for the machine hours operated.

Material Cost Variance

"The actual cost of materials consumed is obtained in the customary way, and the standard cost of the standard quantities specified is computed by extending reports of production". (p. 888.)

"The story therefore as to materials is that 114.4% of the quantity specified was used at 98% of the cost". (p. 889.)

Possibly such "typical cost data" as these may be "of practical help in the solution of the problems of management"; and possibly they prove that the "standard costs" system is so much more adequate than the individual manufacturing-order system; but I am going to contend that exactly the contrary of the latter proposition is the simple truth. I believe we have got to get back to original facts and that we have had no business to get so far away from them. I am going to describe very briefly what the individual manufacturing-order cost system is, but first I am going to make a few quotations from the other papers, all (as I have said) by stanch advocates of the "standard costs" system.

"It is obvious that these variances—the difference between the standard and actual scrap made, not including any spoiled or defective work—must be reported by kinds of materials, by departments or operations on which the scrap is made". (p. 901).

"Variances must be reported by departments and by operations, and in some instances it will be advisable to classify them by kinds of product. This is not a difficult task, because obviously it is advisable and in many cases necessary to know just how each workman is performing, and since this must be determined from the individual work tickets, it is only a question of sorting and tabulating variances from individual tickets". (p. 904.)

15

"It is not enough just to establish standards, and incorporate them in the costs. They must be constantly studied and since standards are of no value unless there is an attempt to live up to them, the variances must be the subject of constant analysis and study. Then it follows that if they are to be analysed and studied they must be presented in a way to bring out the essential facts". (p. 908.)

"If the results can not be traced back to individuals responsible for those results, if the performance can not be definitely assigned as to responsibility to an individual, then the main purpose of the cost accounts to give control is lost". (p. 1245).

"Variances are analysed and reported in full detail so as to determine the real cause and individual responsibility for them." (p. 1259).

There is no doubt that these quotations describe what must ultimately be accomplished, if there is to be an effective check upon the economy of manufacture. Variances in scrap produced must be identified by operations, and variances in labor costs must be identified by operations, and so on with all other variances. The work must be limited to variances that matter, and nothing that really matters must be overlooked. One needs in the first place a convenient indication where something has developed that deserves attention. One is not going to subject every stores order and every labor ticket to a critical examination, and on the other hand it is a poor starting point merely to know that something is wrong somewhere in the cost of a considerable number of orders (even if they are of one "product class") in a considerable division of time. It seems to me unquestionable that the single manufacturing order, or sub-order, is the most convenient unit to disclose and give the initial approximate location of any excessive cost. The form and ruling of the cost ledger, giving the original cost account in fairly well analized shape, help very greatly. I do not know where there are equal advantages, even in this single respect, in any other procedure.

In trying to indicate what, in this one respect, factory accounting which includes individual cost accounts for manufacturing or construction orders is, I shall add little or nothing to what is either in Garcke & Fells' *Factory Accounts* (1887) or in my own articles in this JOURNAL August, 1906, to January, 1907.

As to materials, first. It is too late to begin to secure economy in these when they are issued to the shops to be used in manufacture, and in saying this I am not referring to purchase prices. I

16

am referring to the quantities purchased and the times of purchasing. The need is that the quantities shall be sufficient and not excessive for specific and standard requirements, and that the times of purchasing shall be such that the shop orders shall be filled promptly upon presentation to the storehouse. Accounting control, beginning with the purchase invoices, must be established, for this is double-entry factory bookkeeping. And effective physical control of stores must be created, or there will be troubles which the accounts will disclose, but which ought never to occur.

The departments here involved are the engineering department, the purchasing department and the stores department. The stores department is naturally the centre, and the stores ledgers are the essential instrument. The sequences of the accounts in the stores ledgers are of a good deal of importance, for convenience of working and of observation. Every account for materials and supplies, stocks of which are to be regularly maintained, is headed with a stock limit and standard order, established and revised as necessary by the engineering department. This, of course, applies to all operating supplies, and to all supplies and parts for plant repairs, as well as to materials which enter into the products; for factory accounting is as closely concerned with the economizing of factory capacity, the avoidance of idle machine time from any cause (as for instance the lack of promptness and speed in repairs), as it is with economy in the use of materials or direct labor.

The storehouse is furnished with lists of materials for all orders to be manufactured, and columns are provided in the stores-ledger form to enter these in the respective accounts. If these appropriations of materials reduce the free stocks below the stock limits, then the storehouse issues requisitions upon the purchasing department. These requisitions are noted in the stores ledger accounts. They may be subject to the O.K. of the engineering department, which is thus given the opportunity to raise any question which any changing conditions may suggest. A copy of the actual purchase order is furnished to the storehouse and noted in the stores ledgers with date of contracted delivery. The storehouse as well as the purchasing department watches deliveries for any lateness and need to trace. The storehouse is responsible for using every means now in its possession to insure the prompt filling of shop orders and the maintenance of free stocks in accordance with the engineering department standards in force.

17

Each shop has its own series of stores orders, and each series is consecutively numbered. They are summarized on sheets upon which the two final figures of the numbers are printed consecutively. When the summaries are closed at the end of the month, the blanks show the unfilled shop orders. The extent to which the storehouse is fulfilling its purpose of filling the shop orders without delay is plainly visible. Inactive stocks are plainly visible in the stores ledger accounts.

A cost account is kept for each manufacturing or construction order. If the order is divided into sub-orders, there must be the same division in the estimates, or in the standard costs sheets for standard products. The cost-ledger forms are ruled with all the columns necessary to facilitate comparisons between actual costs and previous calculations. The original stores orders for materials may be kept sorted by manufacturing orders. No excessive use of materials, defective materials or spoiled work can be obscured. Usually, if not always, these things are disclosed both in the material comparisons and in the labor comparisons of which I shall speak presently. We are dealing now with original facts, where they occur, and not with far-off percentages of variance.

And as to labor. It is very simple to summarize the direct labor on each manufacturing order, or sub-order, each payroll period. This is done, on a form provided for the purpose, from a weekly labor sheet kept for each workman. The original labor tickets are also kept sorted by manufacturing orders. When a manufacturing order is completed the total of the direct labor is compared with the same in the standard cost or estimate, and the comparison and all the original labor tickets and summaries are passed on to a man who is not an accountant, but who has knowledge and experience of shop practice, who should conduct a continuous scrutiny of direct labor costs, whose department is organized for this purpose. This is all a part of the practice in connection with individual manufacturing-order cost accounts, as I have myself seen it in operation.

I come to what I suppose I must call "burden." It is intimated in more than one paper that the treatment of these expenses (i. e., all expenses other than materials and direct labor) is practically the same with the "standard costs" system as it is with individual manufacturing-order cost accounts. I am not willing to subscribe to this. In fact, very far from it.

18

Mr. Camman says (p. 874): "The burden rates are the budgeted costs divided between machine hours, man hours, or other measures of time occupied in the manufacturing processes." Closely similar quotations could be made from the other papers and discussions.

In the first place, as I remarked in my September article, not all expenses outside of materials and direct labor are, or are to be called, burden. Under certain conditions, no doubt, all of these expenses may be ascertained in their respective totals, and combined, and distributed to the costs of products (subject to any distributions to factory capacity not operated) by a uniform method. But where the manufacturing operations have a large and varied character, and this very definitely includes the larger machine shops, engineering works, and steel works, such a method is quite inapplicable. Power must have its own cost accounts, both for control of its costs and for any correct distribution of the expense. Fuels must be recorded as consumed for particular purposes, and wherever they are consumed in large quantities, the possibilities of standards of consumption are to be fully examined. Very largely the more expensive tools must be direct charges to the cost accounts for the products for which they are made, either in total immediately or by gradual amortization. The reduction of all the manufacturing expenses, not chargeable direct to products, to expenses of production centres (of which the machine tool with its hourly rate is one example) is in many cases the only possible way to arrive at practically true cost figures.*

I will close this part of the subject of this article with two general criticisms.

First: In these extended discussions of "standard costs" there is, I believe, no indication of, no reference to, any difference in types of cost accounts whether they are for the manufacture of fountain pens or locomotive engines, boxes of stationery or an electrical installation; always standard costs and always no "job-order cost accounts." Always a single instrument instead of instruments very varied, to be availed of, or often by a simple process discovered rather than invented, to meet whatever conditions there are. For it is the character of the operations that must determine the pattern of the accounts. This is true in the machine

---

*In relation to the various expenses included in "burden" it will not be unprofitable to bear in mind A. Hamilton Church's *Production Factors*, and David Moffat Myers' *Factory Power Plants*, and a number of articles on power costs in the *Engineering Magazine* (or *Factory & Industrial Management*) in the past few years.

19

industries, and it is even more simply true in the chemical and metallurgical industries, where a flow-sheet of the material practically gives, or may be directly translated into, the plan of the operating ledger. The two must correspond, step by step. A simple illustration is the cost accounts for an industrial power plant. It is the chart of the generation and conversion centres, and transmission lines, and meters, that gives the series of accounts through which is accomplished the distribution of all costs to the departments, and often units of equipment, using the power in any forms.

Second: It seems to me that, from the first, the proponents of the "standard costs" system, captivated I suppose by a sense of new discovery, have ignored everything that was done in the work of estimating and cost accounting by all the factory accountants and others who were before them, who thought and worked in the same field. And it seems to me that they continue to do so. Hence in these papers and discussions much attempted disparagement of all work other than their own. To such expressions I will not further refer, but I will take one statement seriously and simply made.

The chairman of the session of the 1929 international congress for the day devoted to cost-accounting discussion, himself an officer of the National Association of Cost Accountants, said (*Proceedings*, p. 1219): "Twenty-five years ago, cost accounting, or as we prefer to call it industrial accounting, was not in existence. The first books in this country were written just about twenty-five years ago and the literature before that time was very scarce." And yet Suplee's *Mechanical Engineer's Reference Book* (Lippincott, 1904) says (p. 787) "Valuable works upon the subjects of works management and cost keeping are the following: J. Slater Lewis' *Commercial Organization of Factories*, Arnold's *Complete Cost Keeper*, Arnold's *Factory Manager and Accountant*, Garcke & Fells' *Factory Accounts*, Matheson's *Depreciation of Factories*, and Metcalfe's *Cost of Manufactures*. Even this list did not include A. Hamilton Church's "Proper Distribution of the Expense Burden," which appeared in the *Engineering Magazine* in 1901.

And before quite closing this part of my subject I return for a moment to the quotation from the article of December, 1908, which is made the starting point of the "standard costs" system. In it, it was claimed first that the existing practice omitted the

20

calculation of costs before manufacture; and second, that the determination upon completion of manufacture was "wholly and absolutely incorrect." As to the first, I have shown conclusively that there was no such omission; and as to the second Mr. Camman, at least, returns completely to actual recorded costs for the purposes of inventories, profit-and-loss accounts and balance-sheets. And these are the same actual costs except that they are certainly rendered somewhat less accurate individually by ascertaining them for "product classes" and reducing them to individual product costs by averaging the differences between the actual costs and the previous calculations; and they are certainly rendered less accurate by throwing expenses of the most various character together and distributing them all as burden. Still, far from regarding them as "wholly and absolutely incorrect," Mr. Camman uses them as true figures for the ultimate purposes of the accounts. It is proper to add that other advocates of the "standard costs" system dissent from Mr. Camman's procedure in this respect. Being skeptical of actual records, they seem to have perfect faith in the infallibility of calculations of individual product costs which are never tested by comparisons with actual individual product cost accounts. For my own part, I believe that as far as the previous calculations are sound and correct, and with the accounting control of factory expenditures as nearly as possible perfected, the differences between prior calculations and subsequently determined costs could be but small, inasmuch as the cost of idle facilities, and variations of indirect expenses from standards which are necessarily used for these in all cost accounts, and the costs of errors and accidents and certain inefficiencies (I have in mind particularly power wastes above normal allowances), should all be separately stated and carried direct to the profit and loss account.

But there is another aspect of the "standard costs" system. I mentioned it at the beginning of this article when I said that from its emphasis on the prior calculation of costs, there had emerged a plan for supplementary wages (completing the remuneration of factory labor), which would substitute a profound common interest for the narrow individual interests fostered by existing wage incentive schemes.

I will take this suggestion as it is expressed in the paper by Mr. C. R. Stevenson of New York, and I will try to develop the possibilities in it a little independently; for while the matter is alluded

21

to not only in Mr. Stevenson's paper but elsewhere in these papers and discussions, there is apparently no attempt anywhere in them to treat it fully.

Mr. Stevenson is enumerating certain features of modern factory organization and accounts. His third item, stated at some length, is the setting of standards of costs of all sorts. Then follows:

> "Fourth: *Using practically the same standards as provided for in item 3 as a basis,** our next step is to set up incentive schemes whereby those who are responsible for operations will automatically share in the savings made."

For the space of a generation or more we have heard and known of wage incentive schemes and profit-sharing systems and bonuses. The first have been concerned, almost although not quite exclusively, with direct labor upon products, and almost always they operate to affect the wages of the workmen merely individually. They isolate the interests of each workman, and deepen his concentration on his individual job; and further they leave unaffected, at any rate for any good, a very large percentage of the whole working force. The labor of auxiliary departments, whatever they may be; the maintenance of the plant; the generation and transmission of power—all these and still other classes of labor have usually been outside of the operation of such schemes, and if these have resulted in greater efficiency of working, we have known that there was always a vast field to which their influence did not extend.

We have probably all of us considered plans by which this might be remedied, and more or less we have attempted it. In some industries the problem was comparatively simple, and in others it remained difficult. For long no general scheme that might be applied in the machine industries was, I believe, anywhere apparent.

Profit-sharing plans have aimed to secure supplementary wages to all employees impartially, but there has been the very great objection that the result depended on influences beyond the control of any employees, and very obviously outside the sphere of the factory.

In many industries there has been an attempt to offer all employees impartially the opportunity to earn something, and something very substantial, beyond immediate wages, namely pensions at retiring ages. That this should, at least in manufacturing in-

*Italics are mine.—J. W.

22

dustry, ever operate impartially or be effective except as to a moderate percentage of all the people employed, must always have been more than doubtful. But the attempt has been at least an acknowledgment that something substantial might be earned, ought to be earned, beyond wages at the levels which have existed.

The "standard costs" system contemplates that there shall be calculations of inclusive costs, prior to manufacture, or apart from the records of actual manufacture, for *all* production. It is to be assumed that these shall be as perfect as possible in all respects to represent complete economy of manufacture, fairly attainable. Not economy of working here and there, but absolutely everywhere; in the saving of materials, in efficiency of labor, in power costs, in maintenance costs, in the operation of every auxiliary department, in the utilization of factory capacity as far as work is provided therefor, and in perfection of product. This is not to be attained through the exclusive concentration of every employee on his individual job. It requires the perfecting of organization, and the coöperation of the whole force working together with a single aim.

The "standard costs" system, then, takes these calculations as a basis for a supplementary wage plan. It seems to be indicated that the additional wages are paid only to the more important employees, those upon whom responsibilities more conspicuously rest. If this is the meaning, I think it is only a first step. The appeal must be to the working forces as a whole and impartially. It is not even so much a matter of a common money interest as it is a matter of a single spirit.

I will not here attempt to outline exact procedure, which, however, is no difficult matter. The essential thing is that the total of the standard costs for the actual production, and the total of the actual costs for the same be used as factors in the determination of the measure of actual economy in the total operations, and that according to this measure, an additional equal percentage upon all wages, from the wages of the works manager to the wages of the humblest of what is called common labor, be paid.

As far as my understanding and judgment go, and my understanding may be incomplete and my judgment may be erring, this is the single contribution of the "standard costs" system to factory accounting and factory economy, and to the possibilities of higher wages with lower costs of products. But even if it is a single contribution, I believe it to be of supreme value.

23

For Product Safety Concerns and Information please contact our EU
representative GPSR@taylorandfrancis.com
Taylor & Francis Verlag GmbH, Kaufingerstraße 24, 80331 München, Germany